M

TIME,

LESS

STRESS

🎔 *Visit the Piatkus website!*

Piatkus publishes a wide range of best-selling fiction and non-fiction, including books on health, mind, body & spirit, sex, self-help, cookery, biography and the paranormal.

If you want to:
- read descriptions of our popular titles
- buy our books over the internet
- take advantage of our special offers
- enter our monthly competition
- learn more about your favourite Piatkus authors

VISIT OUR WEBSITE AT: www.piatkus.co.uk

Copyright © 2002 by Judi James

First published in 2002 by
Judy Piatkus (Publishers) Limited
5 Windmill Street
London WIT 2JA
e-mail: info@piatkus.co.uk

This edition published in 2003

The moral right of the author has been asserted

A catalogue record for this book is available from the British Library

ISBN 0-7499-2455-4

Text design by Paul Saunders
Edited by Jan Cutler

This book has been printed on paper manufactured with respect for the environment using wood from managed sustainable resources

Typeset by Phoenix Photosetting, Chatham, Kent
Printed and bound by Bookmarque Ltd, Croydon

MORE
TIME,
LESS
STRESS

How to create
two extra hours every day

Judi James

PIATKUS

Contents

Introduction

Q: Can I *really* create an extra two hours every day, or is this another one of those big-claim books, like 'How to Eat More and Lose Weight' or 'How to Be Rich Without Any Effort'?

A: Anyone can create more perceptual time in their day (obviously you can't suddenly decide to run to a 26-hour clock). You could do it tomorrow, if you wanted, in just two simple steps:

1. Stop doing some things.

2. Start doing other things smarter.

Easy? Of course not, which is why I wrote this book. You will tell yourself there are things you *can't* stop doing because your very life depends on them. This might be true of breathing and eating but – generally – those two actions don't take up too much of your time (unless you're on the 'How to Eat More and Lose Weight' diet, that is). Anything else can usually be jettisoned without your name getting in the papers for murder or suicide.

So you *can* cut down.

Then there are probably a few things you could do better as well, like travelling, shopping or shuffling paperwork. This book aims to help you cut back on the unnecessary stuff by:

1. Reprioritising your life.

2. Thinking smarter, so that your brain is tackling tasks at maximum efficiency.

3. Providing short, sharp tips to help cut down on time wastage in general. Its scope is unlimited. It will help you plug time leaks throughout your entire life, not just in the workplace.

Believing in Fairies

The success of your time tweaking will depend on two major factors, though, and you need to know them before you dip into this book:

Time-management techniques only work if you believe in them

They are the Tinkerbell of the self-help market. Remember Peter Pan? How Tinkerbell nearly dies when the children stop believing in fairies? Trying to time-save at half-cock won't work. You need to be committed. You need to *believe* creating extra time in your day is possible. Your life can change, but only if you let it. If you *think* time management won't work then you will only try it enough to prove yourself right.

You need to see what you are going to do with your newly created extra time

If you are going to create gaps then you must know how you plan to fill them. Otherwise those time gaps fill up with the same type of stuff you worked hard to dig out in the first place. I call this Digging a Hole in the Sand. Keep the image in mind because we will be using it a lot later on.

Q: Who needs this book?

A: This book is aimed at anyone who wants more hours in the day and that – in my experience – means everyone.

Remember: bad time management can be a killer!

You know the scenario: you work too hard achieving too little. You forget how to relax. You get stressed. You keel over. You die.

The Cult of *Karoshi*

Are you overworked? In Japan they have a medical term for working yourself to death. The word is: *karoshi*. Write it on a Post-it and stick it somewhere you can see it. Being busy is fine, but if you work *too* much you will destroy your life and your health.

Are *you* working yourself to death? Do *you* want to croak your last breath over the photocopier as you attempt to change yet another ink cartridge? Or do you want do die aged 100 in your country mansion, surrounded by family and adoring friends? Of course, the least bad scenario of poor time management is that you forget to have a life.

So, are you convinced yet?

Prepared to believe in fairies? OK, time to get on with the rest of the book.

Your Top Ten Time-Management Tips

Let's cut to the quick and look at your main framework of change if you are to redesign your time in the ways outlined in this book ... the scope of your work is simple:

- You will need to define your life goals.

- And then go on to the smaller, daily objectives.

- You will need to plan a time-vision – how do you intend spending any time saved?

- You will discover whether there are some things that you are doing that are of low-grade importance, i.e. things you can stop doing.

- You will see how to become more time-efficient in the things you either want or *have* to do. To achieve this, you will study theories of brain efficiency and stress management, as well as more 'empowering' skills, like negotiating and assertiveness, and practical skills, like filing and IT management.

So, to save you time straight away, here are my top ten tips for successful time management:

1 Discover your goals

Prioritising time is impossible if you have no idea of your personal life objectives. It's a little like trying to plan a journey with no destination in mind.

2 Change the script

Your intra-personal dialogues will be an important factor in your success. You need to think clearly, calmly and positively. Eliminate negative stress and worry, and emotional baggage, and allow your brain to function effectively for a change.

3 Stop moaning and start doing

I don't want to calculate the hours lost per week in whingeing because I know the results would be terrifying, and especially depressing when the moans are mostly about how busy you are.

4 Say 'No'

Somewhere back in time you agreed to that extra workload. You could have refused but you decided to become a martyr instead. Learn to renegotiate. Become assertive instead.

5 Take breaks

You work through your lunch break – why, exactly? So you can finish early? Who are you kidding? Get out, get some air and use the time to take stock and re-energise instead.

6 Focus and time-lock

Find out how to train your brain to work in the here and now.

7 Tidy up

You're going to achieve a balanced lifestyle. You're going to learn how to become a clean-up obsessive at work but a housework slacker at home.

8 Grapple with the workplace Time Bandits

Like meetings, for instance. To the keen time-manager, meetings are the Antichrist. They eat away at your day until you forget what the hell you went to work for in the first place. Learn how to take control of these and other time-wasters.

9 Communicate clearly

Get it right first time. Make people understand you. Waffling, using jargon, dropping hints or straying off the point are all time-expensive habits. Get good at briefing other people. Clear communication leads to understanding which leads to effective action.

10 Have fun

Fun keeps the brain fit. Worry equals brain waste. And remember – if you don't have fun, why bother?

Time States

This book has been constructed in a style to fit in with your four main 'time states'. When you are busiest there is a selection of tips that you can skim-read to select stuff you will find useful. The first section focuses on life-changing techniques, like linear thinking, stress management and effective learning styles. Then there is a section of studiable, learnable skills, like concise communications and getting the most out of your PC, that will help long-term planning. The third deals with all those life-saving tips and techniques for life outside the workplace.

Future Perfect?

(Or why information technology and labour-saving devices speeded up the slow jobs but didn't leave us all with time to kill, as it promised.)

It is one of the campaigns of this book to help you make IT time-manager friendly. I believe it to be a Time Bandit, taken overall. I would like you to prove me wrong. It is my belief that IT eats up more time than it saves.

The Way to Go: Reasons Why Modern Life and Business Have Decimated Your Time Management

Time management should not be a modern issue. The problem should be leisure management, i.e. what to do with all our spare time. God (aka Bill Gates) has given us mortals the gift of technology to enable us to reduce our working hours dramatically, yet we still choose to live in an era of overwork and underachievement. Why? Well, there are four main reasons:

1 Post-recession depression

Like survivors of a nuclear war, post-recession workers are constantly on the lookout for the spectre of the next. No one could forget the agonies of 'downsizing' and negative equity. You take little for granted, especially your job, leading to:

2 Presenteeism

You attempt to impress your boss by lashing yourself to the office chair. First one to leave is a sissy.

3 The popularity factor

You keep saying 'yes' to extra work because you want to be liked.

4 Digging a hole

You suffer from the 'Digging a Hole in the Sand' syndrome. When you use IT to create a hole you just fill it with even more work. Read on for further details.

Modern Business Cults

The cult of the hole in the sand

Have you ever dug a hole in soft sand on the beach? The more you dug, the more the sand slipped back in to fill it. The faster you dug the faster the sand slipped. Your parents probably laughed themselves sick as you dug yourself into a frenzy, never really understanding why the hole got no bigger. Then you got irritable and started to cry. This was probably your first introduction to job-related stress.

IT has created your hole in the sand. It makes jobs faster, which should create gaps. Only more jobs keep slipping into those gaps until you have to work yourself into a frenzy just to stay where you are.

E-mail is a perfect example of the Hole in the Sand philosophy in practice. You use it to make communication quicker, but as communication speeds up more people use it and therefore the time you save sending messages is more than made up for by the time spent reading all the messages that people keep sending you.

The cult of competitive busyness

Only the fast survive in modern business. We got busy, then we got busier and now we can't stop. Filling each minute in a meaningful way is semi-compulsive. Your compulsion may spill over into holidays, too. As gaps in our lives shorten, even the rapid becomes unbearable.

The cult of multitasking

We admire the multitasker. When a woman is described as 'having it all' she inevitably holds down a high-flying career while nurturing ten kids and making her own mayonnaise as well.

The cult of the slacker society

The slacker society – the generation who saw work as a necessary evil and revered rest and long breaks – has said goodbye. Now we're hooked on the adrenaline rush of busyitis. We *want* to slow down or stop, but the reality of that ideal gets farther and farther out of our reach.

The cult of fearing wasted hours

Did the cult of work–life balance ever really get off the ground? In my experience, no. Like 'open-door policies' and 'empowerment' it was yet another workplace chimera that fell through the reality gap between theory and practice. Why? Well, flexing time at work to spend more time at home sounded great, but in the end, for many companies, it became yet another burden of guilt for the worker. Bosses skipped the bit that said it was their responsibility and landed it in the laps of the employees. So you were supposed to get a life, just like you were supposed to manage your own stress and manage your own emotions. Some companies got it right: when Microsoft UK asked their staff if they would opt for a shorter day or a big pay rise, six out of ten plumped for the shorter day. Happiness is based on time and how it is spent, not money.

The cult of the workaholic

The complete workaholic martyr may like to know that work effectiveness isn't based on time, either. Staying late doesn't mean doing more. Research in the 1960s proved that output falls back to a standard working week after less than four weeks working continuous overtime.

You will need to create time to stop and think now and again

Warning: Terminal Pressure

No one can improve your time management if your pressure is terminal. Changes in lifestyles have added extra burdens on nearly everyone's time. These include:

- ◆ Downsizing
- ◆ Empowerment

- Global commitments

- Both partners in a relationship expected to have a career

- Faster pace of life.

Now, one thing you have to remember: if you do two people's jobs at work; if you run a business and a large family; if you take on everything life has to throw at you without remembering to cut some slack in other areas, the simple basics of time management will be near to useless for you. Your diary can be ordered, your to-do lists comprehensive, your filing well organised but you will still be too busy to cope.

Your workplace time-management techniques are going to have four major areas of focus:

1. Routine – creating 'to-do' lists etc.

2. Systems – using IT.

3. Planning – setting goals, prioritising and increasing competence.

4. Balancing – your social, intellectual and physical needs and well-being with your schedule of work demands.

So, now you've grazed through some of the current problems, and presumably identified with one or two along the way, how are you going to start making it all right?

Well, the first and possibly most important step has to be taking an objective view of your life right now. Turn yourself into a wiser, less emotional being and look at your frenzied, ant-like existence. Given that the busy person you are studying only gets the one life, then how stupidly is it spending most of its time? Start to think how you would like your life to be. Start to plan bigger priorities and goals. And yes, this book will help you to start.

Big Picture Time Management

I said at the start of the book that to manage your time you can just stop doing some things. For instance, if you decided to cut your sleep time in half you could make four more hours in any day. But you'd be knackered, of course.

So, before you start snipping, ask yourself the big question:

What things are important to me?

First and foremost be guided by your final destination, not your route. Where do you want your life to go? What do you want it to look like? Paring off minutes and hours here and there to store in another pot will be of little use unless you can see the glorious landscape of your overall life's plan. Why? Well, because to be an effective time-manager you will need to:

Heal at source

Start with the big stuff and end with the small, clean-up tips. Tidying your desk may make your life look a bit better but you need to start by tidying your mind of its clutter and focusing on your priorities.

First you will need to see what is most precious to you. Only then can you start pruning.

Warning: Don't turn into a time obsessive

Never over-plan your life. Pack a schedule too tight and you create order that is destructive. No one can live happily dominated by the clock. You are creative and you are a free spirit. You work well with pressure, goals and deadlines but you also need some time to go into free-fall. If you don't you will never realise your potential. Give yourself a break now and again.

Goal definition

How many roles do you expect to fulfil in your life? What are your personal goals and expectations? What are your personal priorities?

What Are You Going to Do Next?

Identify the most important things in your life and prioritise work and time loads around them.

Written Exercise: Planning Your Objectives

Why do you want to create more time? Answer this before you go any further. Write the answer down. The title of the book tempts you with the offer of two more hours per day. Two additional hours means cutting back considerably on your present behaviour. But what is your aim in gaining those hours? Is it:

◆ To free up work-task time so that you have more time for recreation?

◆ To free up work-task time so that you have more time for more work tasks?

The difference is enormous. It relates directly to your overall level of satisfaction with this book. If you spend your freed time leisurely you'll have time to acknowledge its effectiveness. If you use it to add to your current tasks you may feel it hasn't worked at all. You'll be back to that Hole in the Sand again.

Tasks grow to fit time. If you want to free some of your time tasks to deal with others that are closer to your values, plan with that in mind.

Creating a Time Vision

Why more time, then? What do you want to do more of? What are your personal priorities? Use the next page to get some overall aims in your life. Ask yourself:

◆ What do I plan to do with my extra time?

◆ Do I need to redesign it to cope with the work I have?

◆ Am I hoping to leave the office on time for a change?

◆ Is my career the main motivation factor in my life?

◆ Do I enjoy targets and tasks or the companionship of others?

◆ Do I want to work harder, smarter, or less?

◆ Do I get turned on by money or praise or helping others?

◆ Do I live to work or work to live?

Are you a corporate ratpacker?

Don't get all gooey about the work–life balance stuff if you know the reality is not really you. Do you want to spend more time playing with the kids/chatting with your husband/romping with the dog? Or do you go to work to get away from the boredom of those very tasks? How are you at Christmas or on holiday? Do you relish every minute or do you find yourself praying for some workplace emergency that might call you back to your laptop?

Hobbies, sports, diets, degree courses and family outings can all sound great until you start doing them. Think long and hard. Many people are happiest at work. 'Live to work' is well within their comfort zone. Business is recruiting more and more of these corporate ratpackers every year. Once we just ate at our desks. Now we can do everything apart from give birth there.

The PC provides us with access to the entire world from our workstations.

- We meet our partners in the workplace (well 40 per cent of us do, anyway).

- We make social and best friends there.

- We can shop there, on-line.

- We can even die there (one poor proof-reader in Scandinavia sat unspotted for several days, having died in harness).

- We can drink and boogie on down there if our company is one of the many that provides a bar facility.

For many workers, out-of-hours life has lost its appeal. Corporate jargon makes them difficult to understand anywhere outside the office building.

You may be one of these corporate ratpackers. Make sure you know before you start shooting off to Disneyland Paris with a vanload of kids.

Goals and Values

Take a couple of sheets of paper and answer the questions below before you make a seriously bad call.

My core values in life are:
I am happiest doing:
I feel guilty about:
My roles in life are: (i.e. parent, partner, son/daughter, boss, employee, dog owner, etc.)

My emotional priorities are:
My key task priorities are:

My life:
Looking at your current situation, create a breakdown of
time percentages, listing all the different departments of

your life and how much time is spent, on average, in each one, i.e.:

♦ Work 61 per cent

♦ Commuting 6 per cent

♦ Drinking in pub 10 per cent

♦ Relaxing at home 20 per cent

♦ Shopping 3 per cent

♦ Etc.

My ideal:
Now plan out a list of ideal times, broken down into percentages, spent on these and other pursuits. Feel free to include any ideal tasks that you are currently not doing.

Make your wish lists realistic; make sure your values and goals marry in with your targets.

Time Lords

Once you start to study these time goals you can begin to give them a name: Time Lords. Time Bastards are the things that prevent you from tackling a task in a time-economical way. Then there are the Time Bandits, people and events that leap into the breech, becoming non-important priorities.

Time Lords will be your day to day and life priorities. They are the things you have pledged to give maximum effort into achieving. Time Lords will be why you are learning to manage your time, so that you can donate the surplus to them.

One last question before you embark on the next stage: what do you think will happen to your life at work if you manage your time well enough to create spaces?

- ◆ You will get a rise from the boss.

- ◆ You will become more popular.

- ◆ You will be awarded employee of the month.

- ◆ You will be given more work from the boss.

Be careful!

Types of Time: Real Time v Perceptual Time

Time is a smug-faced constant. It comes and it goes. You can't really stretch it. We know the logic of measured time. But we also know the clock tells lies. An hour spent waiting for a train bears no conceivable relation to an hour spent drinking with friends. So your time has to be measured in two ways so that you can calculate your personal use of it and start making any adjustments: real time and perceptual time.

Perceptual time

This can be broken down into several subheadings. The best way to understand the concept is to compare twenty minutes spent in a changing room trying on clothes with the same twenty minutes spent waiting outside the changing room while your partner tries on clothes. The time span is exactly the same in reality, but perceptually the two experiences are incomparable. Your partner's twenty minutes may feel like ten but your's might seem like the best part of an eternity.

In the workplace especially there are many varied ways of measuring regular patterns of perceptual time, the most common being:

Nanotime

This is the swiftest-moving stuff of the lot. Nanotime is either panic time or enjoy time. Nanotime can last for less than a second or an entire day. An entire day spent in nanotime will feel as though it has lasted less than a second. Ways to spend nanotime include:

◆ Rushing to finish a proposal by 5.30 pm.

◆ Trying to set up PowerPoint on you laptop before the audience starts arriving.

◆ Trying to get the job-seeker/dating agency/porno website off your screen when you see the boss approaching.

◆ Shopping at lunchtime.

◆ Any work done close to an urgent deadline. As the deadline approaches, nanotime speeds up.

◆ Reading a riveting novel on the tube.

Kill time

This is the slowest time of the lot. One minute of kill time equals approximately one week of real time. This can be spent:

◆ Queuing for *anything*, although supermarket and ticket queues deserve their own special place in the hall of fame.

◆ Waiting for a lift.

◆ Waiting on hold on the phone.

◆ Any train or plane journey where you forget to take a book or magazine.

◆ Waiting for the bill after a dull business lunch.

Hurry time

This is the disproportionate stuff. Hurry time covers the bits you lose track of, usually because you are too stressed to have the ability to measure it. It lives in a self-contained bubble, with barely any connection to the real world. It can be:

- ◆ Waiting desperately for a toilet cubicle to become free.

- ◆ Waiting for the taxi or train doors to unlock when you are rushing to make a connection.

- ◆ Waiting for your eyes to focus as you try to read that letter telling you whether you got the job or not.

Gone time

These can be rare in modern business. They are the lowest of the lows, moments when you reach such an intense level of boredom or depression that you lose the will to live. Often these lows are fluctuations, dictated by the pace of the rest of your work. If you are normally employed on a 'flat-out' basis then it will not take much for you to dip acutely. Attention spans get shorter in modern life. We expect constant diversion or entertainment and anything else is hard to endure. I once worked in a shop that had few customers. The highlight of the day was dusting the shelves, and I would eke this job out as long as possible to ward off the defining moment between 'very bored' and 'brain-dead'. Gone time occurs when you:

- ◆ Hear your boss criticise your work or behaviour and wait through the dazed pause for the pain of hurt pride to kick in.

- ◆ Deliberate in Starbuck's between a tall or grande latte.

- ◆ Watch the slow-mo moment as the same cup of coffee hangs in the air before spilling over your keyboard.

Mean time

Mean time is when your working day passes by at its normal rate. This may be comfortable or uncomfortable, but to you it is the common average. This time could be logged on a graph, showing peaks and troughs at certain times of the day, or it could emerge as a straight line of flat-out activity.

Dead time

When nothing is doing – nothing at all.

Time Skilling

One in six office staff would rather spend an hour playing solitaire than be seen to be the first to go home, according to research by Microsoft.

The Top Twenty Time-wasters at Work

The average workplace is awash with Time Bandits and Time Bastards. They survive and thrive in most cultures, mainly because they *are* the culture, but big-scale businesses tend to specialise in them. Easy jobs become complex. Direct communication with one person can take weeks to arrange. One colleague who wanted to speak to another in the same firm was told by his colleague's PA that she could fit him in for a phone conversation at 8.00 am the following Friday.

Good ideas fester and die through lack of implementation. Empowerment was intended to bridge the gulf but ended up being meaningless as most staff were still wary of the boundaries of their accountability.

Companies have become top-heavy. There are too many managers living in too many meeting rooms and not enough out there managing. Corporate theorising is of limited use. Business success rarely fits a pattern. Most bosses would be best employed getting out into the workplace and talking to the staff and seeing how things work, or not, for themselves. Most of the wisdom is already there, it's just that no one is listening. To be an effective time-manager you will need to be aware of your own areas of time leakage. To set the ball rolling, here is a list of some of the most common ones in the workplace:

- ◆ Interruptions, like the telephone.

- ◆ Meetings.

- ◆ Changed goal posts.

- ◆ No daily plan.

- ◆ Prevarication.

- ◆ Laziness.

- ◆ Unwanted e-mails.

- ◆ Chatting to colleagues.

- ◆ Indecision.

- ◆ Equipment breakdown.

- ◆ Hunting for information.

- ◆ Office politics.

- ◆ Waiting for people who are late.

- ◆ Chaotic desk.

- ◆ Lack of delegation.

- ◆ Trying to find people.

- ◆ Saying 'Yes' to everything.

- ◆ Starting jobs but not finishing them.

- ◆ Checking on others.

- ◆ Starting jobs without planning them.

- ◆ Being tired.

There are, of course, many others causes of time leakage, like:

Problems

Yes, problems take time to resolve. They make us think and make us work and achieve. The only *problem* with problems is that we have strange ways of dealing with them. There are two ways to deal with a problem:

1 Sort it

Create a plan or strategy. Evaluate your options. Even decide to let it drop. Or:

2 Moan about it

Weep, wail, wring your hands. Whinge. Wonder 'Why me?' Do nothing to solve the problem.

Which route sounds best to you? Life isn't always fair in its distribution of problems. But you can be sure moaning will only make it worse.

Solution Thinking

Whingeing about your problems is comfortable. Finding solutions requires action and, sometimes, risk and hard work. Which makes us solution-phobic. You will know if you suffer from solution-phobia if you are aware of, or have been told by friends or colleagues, the solution to your dilemma, but you still find reasons to avoid using it. You prefer to moan.

Move Out of Moan Patterns of Behaviour

Stop it right now. Take responsibility for your problems as well as your good fortune. Put yourself in control of your life and your thinking. If that takes massive change then go ahead and start right now.

Meeting Problems With Solutions – 'Sorting it'

Take the problem with time as an example:

♦ Ask yourself: how much more time do I want in the day? An hour? Two hours?

♦ Now create a worksheet: how can I achieve that extra time?

♦ Write down five solutions right away.

♦ Read them through. Do you like them? Would they work?

Fill your worksheet with solutions as you read through this book. The point is you *can* create more time in your day – or the appearance of it, at least.

What you now need to work out is HOW.

PART ONE

Personal Skills

CHAPTER ONE

How to Create Effective Thinking

'Nobody can do two things
at the same time and do them well.'
DON MARQUIS

┌─ *Quick Tips* ──────────────────────────┐

- ◆ Define the best times of the day and week that your
  brain works at peak performance.

- ◆ Define times that your brain works better creatively or
  logically.

- ◆ Define the conditions that will help that process.

- ◆ Get rid of distractions.

- ◆ Provide stimulus by identifying objectives and
  motivations.

- ◆ Offer your brain rewards.

- ◆ Set ten minute targets of high-energy brain activity.

- ◆ Create physical and mental rituals to crank your brain
  into action and to keep the momentum going.

└──────────────────────────────────────┘

◆ Exercise your brain by doing puzzles and learning at least one new thing per day. Build it like a muscle.

◆ Get out of the regular brain patterns. Think outside your box.

◆ Build confidence. Tell yourself you are good at things.

◆ Create brain and memory triggers.

If your brain worked more consistently at peak performance you would create two new hours in any day without the need of other time-management techniques. The problem with the brain, though, is that in the workplace it tends to resemble a car that is just 'ticking over', rather than a well-maintained engine that is purring along at top speed.

Why the inefficiency? Well, there are several reasons, the main ones being:

• Overload
• Stress
• Tiredness
• Boredom
• Poor diet
• Lack of breaks
• Bad habits
• Bad education
• Emotional involvements
• Anxiety
• Lack of focus
• Lack of clear goals
• Lack of relevant goals
• Non-specific communication processes
• Lack of input of correct knowledge
• Reliance on 'tools'
• Culture of 'away from' thinking

- Culture of thinking that is either too global (big picture) or too linear (short-term only)
- Lack of motivation and reward
- Bad working conditions and environment
- Lack of brain 'work-out'
- Illness
- Hangover
- Depression

So What Are Your Brain Objectives?

Hopefully:

- Clarity of thought

- Use of logic

- Ability to access stored knowledge

- Enhanced memory

- Ability to learn quickly.

Ways to Make Your Thinking More Time-Effective

Be clear about your goals

Start with the end in mind. Would you read a map to find a route if you had no idea where you were going? You brain can be wonderfully creative and problem-solving, but only if it knows what the problem is and where you want it to move towards. Write your objective down and then let it get stuck in.

Focus and time-lock

The brain works best when it is absorbed in one task. When you try to multitask it dilutes its effectiveness. Clarity and purity of thought become compromised. Jobs lap over into one another so that you will be half-finishing some and confusing others. There is an emotional overlap, too.

Try to prioritise each task and give it your undivided attention. Finish one before you start another. This may seem to be inefficient behaviour, but it does save you time. If you need to renegotiate, do so. If an urgent call comes in or a client arrives, drop the job you are focused on and transfer that total absorption to the new priority task. Try not to do the new job while keeping your mind on the old one. Cancel and continue.

Focus on the here and now

The mind tends to live in three key time zones: past, present and future. At any given moment you are probably grazing around all three, thinking of something that happened earlier, wondering about something that is going to happen and dealing with present problems all at the same time.

Of all the three key time zones, the one we spend the least time in is the here and now. Focus on the present for clarity and speediness of thought. Drag yourself into the here and now. See past and future thinking as something of a luxury until your task is finished. Remember – you can't change the past, only dwell on it. You can change the future but a lot of future thinking is speculative.

Keep using your brain

Sound obvious? You have about 100 billion brain cells, but what makes you intelligent is the number of connectors between those cells. The more you use your brain the more connections you make between the cells. Like a muscle in your body being pumped up in the gym, you can expand your brain through use. Tune up by increasing brain stimulation. Do quizzes, crosswords and lateral-thinking puzzles and seek out new stimuli to prevent your mind going stale.

I recently trained a young woman who had flunked the telephone stage of a recruitment interview. Why? Because she couldn't spell or add up. The company had tested her on both aspects and she'd been stumped by the simple stuff. Yet she was bright and already holding down a good job. The problem was her education. She had been brought up on spellcheck and calculators. She couldn't do the real thing to save her life. She could only spell if she was gazing at a PC screen. It was the way her brain had been taught to work and respond. Throw some words up on screen and she could do it. Ask her to visualise the word while using the phone and she couldn't.

I told her to do as many crossword puzzles and maths tests as she could before the next interview. There wasn't enough time for her to receive training in both subjects, but there was enough for her to increase accessibility of her already-stored knowledge. She was used to retrieving it in one format. What she had to learn to do was switch to another.

Improve your memory

You have long- and short-term memory. Short term is for things you will only need for a while, possibly a moment. Long term is for things you will need regularly in the future. To remember facts for a long time you need to take them through your short-term memory and into your long-term memory. Steps to improve your memory include:

1. Telling yourself you have a good memory. If you keep repeating the fact you can't remember names etc. this sends self-defeating signals to your subconscious.

2. Learning lists of numbers, like a credit card, PIN or phone number, by creating a sentence that has the same amount of letters in each word, i.e.: A badly lit street can cause danger = 1 5 3 6 3 5 6.

3. Using more than one sense to provide a mental 'print-out' for your brain. If you hear a name, try to 'see' the word as well. Or

create a related picture in your mind. For instance, if you are introduced to a man called Mark Stone, visualise another Mark you know (Mark Fowler from *EastEnders*, for example), holding a large stone in his hand. See the name written above the man's head and repeat the name yourself out loud as soon as possible.

4. Creating a memory trace. We remember mundane details if we can attach them to a memory jogger; i.e., 'I remember meeting the client on that day because it was when I had just come back from a trip to the dentist.' Make your own odd associations to facts or events you want to remember, the odder the better.

5. Remembering with a song. We can recall the words to thousands of songs because the music aids the memory. If you have to remember lists of names, words or places try to set them to a tune.

6. Creating structure. Make lists. Create charts. Write things down. See facts in context with other facts or details. Start to create patterns in your mind. Make lists on Post-its and stick them around your desk so that you glance at them regularly. This can be helpful with names and phone numbers as your subconscious picks them up while you are working.

7. Creating a mnemonic.

8. Creating rhythms. (This is an especially useful technique when you are trying to remember a spelling). An actor learning lines or a dancer learning a complex pattern of steps will have a way of consigning them into long-term memory. Often a rhythm is used as a hook. When I first started dancing and fashion choreography I found it impossible to remember more than three steps because I was trying to learn them in my usual style. Then I found I started linking them to words and/or rhythm. Suddenly it was easier and I found that I could memorise whole blocks without effort. A year ago I was being shown how to play percussion in a steel band. This time I found it difficult to

remember the rhythm patterns, until the tutor told me to attach words to the beats. Suddenly it became easy because I discovered patterns I could hook on to.

Give your brain some breaks

Health and Safety guidelines recommend no more than 20 minutes at a time spent staring at your computer screen. This is not just a matter of ergonomics – the mind needs regular breaks, as well.

Try to work on 20–30 minute blocks of intense, 'peak performance' brain work at a time. Start with 10 minutes of undiluted work and then increase it to 20. The breaks in between need only be short, but remove yourself from your desk or workstation if you can. Take longer breaks for lunch and refreshments. Never eat at your desk. Get an outside break at least once a day. Do something stimulating and different during your breaks, don't just sit staring at the screen saver. Read something funny or relaxing, look at a view out of the window or have a non-work conversation. Time your breaks to avoid them stretching into your work slots.

Manage your stress

New information travels to your middle brain, which in turn passes anything that appears worthwhile up to your conscious, thinking brain. The middle brain also controls your emotions. If there are feelings of fear or anxiety present the new information may never reach your conscious brain. Your mind goes blank.

Identify your different thinking modes

Your brain will be required to flex its style from task to task during the average working day. It's already quite good at coping with all you throw at it but consciously identifying the manner in which you would like it to function will make the transformation process even slicker and help you to give it the tools or environment it needs for enhanced effectiveness.

A Brief Guide to Brain Styles and the Conditions They Need to Perform

1 'Eureka' style

This is the style you'll need to adopt to come up with your greatest, most inspirational thoughts. This is the bit in the detective film where the sidekick slaps his forehead and says: 'Wait a minute, didn't he say the murderer was left-handed? Well, this corpse was shot in the right temple ...' etc. This is the moment the penny drops, the time you think of that name you spent all day hunting for or the solution to that maths puzzle that's been evading you for weeks. Global thinking patterns.

In business: use this style of thinking when you want a new business idea or to remember the name of that client you met four years previously. This is inspirational thinking time.

Conditions: calm, quiet. Don't try this when you are in a hurry. The more pressure you put on your brain the less inspirational your thinking will be. Take yourself away from the workplace, if possible. The mind needs to be in the alpha state (relaxed, half-asleep) for the best thoughts to pop up to the surface. Adrenaline won't help. Meditation will. Close your eyes and relax in your chair. Think of nothing. Allow your brain to graze. Ponder over anything but the problem in hand. Drift on to a higher plain.

For instant inspiration, during a presentation for instance, glance up to the ceiling and slightly to your left. This activates the part of the brain required for instant feedback. I know this upward glance is taught to be taboo by presentation skills trainers who swear by constant eye contact with your audience, but in times of emergency it will have to do. Rub your chin at the same time, to look intellectual, rather than lost. Breathe out. Focus on nothing.

Music to play: relaxation tapes. Repetitive classics. Whale sounds, rainforests, water noise, anything that might take you off to near sleep.

2 Absorbed thought

This style is totally focused, oblivious to all distractions. The task may be devilishly intricate or of a not very high intellectual standard, but just requiring complete attention. Linear thinking, possibly with some global.

In business: anything that may challenge your boredom thresholds or be complex enough to deserve undivided attention. Do this in the workplace if the subject is stimulating, but away from it if attention needs a kick-start.

Conditions: clear the clutter. Tidy your workspace of all distractions. Start with quiet. If the job is interesting you may find background noise less of a problem but if the job is boring try to find a spot with complete silence.

Get rid of any small nagging jobs before you start. Employ any small 'comfort' gestures that will stimulate absorbed attention. Remember what you did as a child when you were reading a good book? If you are alone, feel free to suck your thumb, rock in your seat, twiddle a hank of hair, etc. These 'miracle' touch gestures will help take you back into that state of complete absorption as a reflex. Take your shoes off, if you can, and make yourself feel comfortable. Don't slump into your chair, though. That could take you into the sleep spindles state that will make you too sleepy to concentrate.

Music to play: silence is best.

3 Logical, pragmatic thought – left-brain, analytical functions

This is where you eschew gut reactions and emotive responses and go with the left side of the brain. Mainly linear thinking patterns.

In business: any job that requires you to be logical and sensible. This is the style of reasoned, informed thinking.

Conditions: best done in the workplace. Formal business wear is very much the style for logical, left-brain thinking. If you are in dress-down mode then put on a jacket.

Make your workspace efficient. If things around you are functional and tidy your mind may follow suit. Prepare pens, reams of quality work-paper and any other tools needed to execute your task. Work in lists, graph and chart format. Write headings on sheets of paper to keep you systematic. Keep structure and form, even in your research stage. Use a wall chart, if appropriate. Keep your work clear and understandable. Work as though you are going to have to pass your notes on to a colleague, that way you will be able to make your points clear to yourself.

Sit, but intersperse with bouts of pacing. Sit in a reasonably upright position. Avoid chin-in-hand poses as these tend to stimulate reflective, rather than active, thought.

Music to play: medium-paced. You need to keep momentum. Avoid relaxing or distracting music. What you need is a musical metronome.

4 Research or learning

This is where you need to stimulate the conscious part of the brain as you will be absorbing new information. This is the 'on-your-toes' stuff that will be loading into the subconscious just as soon as the subject is assimilated. Linear and global thinking patterns.

In business: training, learning a new skill, taking in information from one-to-one or group meetings.

Conditions: in or out of the workplace. Medium stimulated. Caffeine may help. Stress-free but not too relaxed physically. Eat snacks and avoid a full stomach. Massage your temples gently. Doodle a little. Move position regularly and take deep breaths. Mouth touching or mouth covering will stimulate a listening, rather than communicating mode. Focus on and become eyes and ears. Close down all 'barrier' emotions, apart from curiosity and excitement. Casual dress, if possible. Fresh air and a desk lamp to focus attention.

Music to play: baroque.

5 Decision-making

This thinking style is reasoned but also possibly gut-reactive. It needs confidence but not arrogance. It should follow style 4, as the decision will come as a result of information gathering.

Decision-making requires big picture thinking, an ability to separate from the linear activities and taking a global look at issues or problems.

In business: from boardroom decisions to the 'shall-I-have-tea-or coffee' stuff.

Conditions: on-the-hoof decisions are difficult to choreograph. Stand still and use just-above-head-height eye focus. Move eyes from left to right, accessing both recalled memory and creative, imaginative sides of brain. This will help you access information to back your decision with both fact and reason and to visualise it being put into practice. Move about, stimulating the brain. Walk, if possible.

Music to play: pacey.

6 Emotional thinking

This is the non-logical, linear thinking that may be necessary for coaching, counselling or dealing with an interpersonal staff issue.

In business: it can involve relationship building with a client or handling an emotive personnel problem.

Conditions: an avoidance of business-related clutter. You are getting back in touch with your more human side that is into relationships, rather than corporate results. Any non-business stimulus might help.

Music to play: relative to emotional situation.

7 Emergency thinking

This is the snap-decision stuff – the sort that defies pragmatics and slow-burners. Some people excel at this and others find it daunting. In a real emergency certain character types will appear to take charge. If the job rests on your shoulders you will need confidence and self-assurance. Dithering is not an option.

In business: fire-fighting on a big or small scale is a constant factor of most modern businesses. Global thinking tends to be put on hold as linear steps come to the fore until the emergency has been dealt with.

Conditions: the fact that you are fire-fighting usually means the conditions will be far from ideal. You need fast-moving, fast-reacting calm. Although the body may be moving and the brain working quickly, there should be calm at the core of the mind.

Separate the mind from the body. Adrenaline will be useful but only if you are in control. Too much and your thinking will tilt over into panic. Soak up enough to keep the brain energised. Move as you think. Make your movements speedy but also smooth and co-ordinated. Avoid rush, as a rushed body translates into rushed thought, which suggests lack of control.

An 'emergency garment' helps stimulate the professional–emergency part of the brain. Obviously you can't don a fluorescent jacket just to deal with a jammed photocopier, but if you can pick up or put on anything 'action-stations' symbolic it will help stimulate the quick-thinking part of the brain.

Music to play: the *Thunderbirds* theme tune is my personal favourite.

8 Creative thinking

Allowing the old creative juices to flow freely can be a difficult option in business, especially if you work in a 'left-brain' environment.

In business: creative thinking may be a necessary facet of a wide variety of tasks, even some that sound purely logical. Just because a job has always been done in one particular way doesn't mean that a more creative strategy might not improve it. Use this style of thinking for creative tasks, like marketing, writing, designing, illustrating, etc., but also for brainstorming, think-tanks and reworking systems and strategies, etc.

Conditions: brainstorming has traditionally been seen to include some sort of communal gathering and sharing of ideas. Psychologists are now concluding that we are potentially more creative in our thinking when working alone. If you feel throwing your ideas into a communal pot with others is stifling your creativity then plan to work alone, particularly in the early stages.

Your environment can be stimulating, especially with semi-related, rather than exclusively related items. Brain-opening may require lateral thinking. If you are working on a housing project, for example, try gathering brain prods from anything with a theme that is different but compatible, like visiting business premises or studying historical maps. Fashion designers are famous for employing any and every source for their clothing ideas, from sporting culture to history. Get yourself to think outside your box by studying lateral subjects.

Work big with your blueprints. Small paper and pens stifle the scope of your ideas. Get the largest sheets possible and fill them. Avoid using your computer when you are in creative-thinking mode. It limits you to its own format. Tapping a keyboard is too left-brain. Right-brainers do it with more artistic, expressive tools, like flip charts and big coloured pens.

Music to play: anything you enjoy. Dip into personal taste.

9 Blends

Of course there will be times when you will need to use blends of the above. Most problems require at least two of the above to solve them effectively. Some may even require:

10 Super blends

Multicombinational thinking. Difficult to pull off, but not if you focus and time-lock on each variety as you need them. Identify the type of thinking needed at any one given moment and avoid wasting time attaching the wrong thinking style to the wrong section of the problem.

Paying Attention

We all go through different levels of attention during the day. These can be identified under six key headings. Reading the page of a book you could move through all six. To be an effective time-manager you need to be able to summon the appropriate attention state at will. They are:

1 Sustained attention

This is the style you will need to stick to a selected task. There is a strong level of absorption here, to the point where you will become unaware of external stimuli that are not associated with your task.

2 Ambient attention

This is where you are applying your attention to a selected stimulus, but are ready to respond to other events. You may be listening to a client during a business function, for instance, while scanning the door for the arrival of another. In attention terms this could be the equivalent to preparing for multitasking. Often the problem is displaying undivided attention to the person speaking, a job most of us find particularly difficult when there are external distractions.

3 Divided attention

This is the true multitasking state. Sometimes we can cope, especially if the multitask is a state we are using regularly, or the skills are compatible, as in driving and talking at the same time. Often we will struggle, though. Try giving a business presentation when you are trying to struggle with a laptop that has crashed.

4 Selective attention

This is where you can choose the task for your attention, while choosing to ignore others. You may be in the middle of one job but able to switch quickly to another before returning to the first.

5 Active attention

You are responding to the stimuli around you, applying useful criteria to the information your senses receive. You are taking in information, responding to stimuli, seeking and evaluating and, subsequently, decision-making.

6 Passive attention

This is where your brain sits back and goes with the flow. It is open but not fully operational. You are in a state of minimum decision- and opinion-making. I often call this 'being drunk'.

Focused Attention

So can you enhance your ability to pay attention? To be an effective time-manager you need the ability to turn on the state of undivided attention at will. To do this you will have to combat both internal and external distractions. Thoughts in your own head will vie for your attention. So will outside stimuli. Try some of the following to focus your attention actively:

◆ Move away from visual stimuli.

◆ If you are at your desk, use books to create side-view 'blinkers', so that you are facing your computer screen at the front, with two temporary screens down either side.

◆ Or, if no one is watching you, place your hands to the sides of your face to form blinkers and to force you to focus in on the job in hand.

◆ Put on spectacles. Before I needed glasses, I had a clear lens pair to put on when I started a job. This made me feel I was dressing up for the job in hand. Reading glasses are good because when you look up you can't focus on anything else around you and tend to go back to your task. Bifocals and half-lenses tend to make you open to interruptions.

◆ Clear any small jobs before you start.

◆ Pick a start and a finish time. Create a contract with yourself: this is the time I will finish and this is not negotiable. This will create the necessary burst of urgency that might stimulate your mind.

◆ Create a visual deadline – have a timer on your desk in front of you.

◆ Go away somewhere and come back to start your job. Go off for a coffee to get your mind warmed up before your sit down at your desk.

◆ Meditate for a few moments.

◆ Write your objective down on a sheet of paper and concentrate on it for a few seconds.

◆ Create a focusing command to trigger your brain's attention. You could use the order 'Focus and time-lock!' or 'Go! Go! Go!' Repeat it to yourself, out loud if possible and be harsh. Beat your brain up a bit. Don't let it meander.

◆ Massage your temples.

◆ Have a sign on your desk saying: 'Please leave me alone'.

◆ Have no other written documents in view as you work.

◆ Hold a pen and work it down the page as you are reading to keep your eyes focused on the relevant lines.

◆ Chew gum.

◆ Don't eat – it distracts the brain.

◆ Caffeine is OK if you're tired but it can make your attention low quality. Avoid alcohol. Green tea is good.

- If you pause to reflect, stare straight ahead. Avoid glancing upward as it tends to stimulate longer musing and creative thinking.

- Have a visual trigger in your line of sight. Make it a list of objectives or a one-word dynamic, written on a page in red ink.

- Tell yourself you have the concentration of a hawk.

- Sit on the edge of your seat.

- Tap your fingers to register impatience and spur the brain.

- Find a point of interest in your subject matter. Boredom is the biggest barrier to concentrated attention.

Self-motivation Techniques

To enhance your focus you will need to first fire yourself up. Many time-management tasks are stupendously boring, and boredom makes the brain and concentration wander. As does disinterest and that general feeling of 'I don't know why I'm doing this'.

What motivates me?

You need to make your objectives in completing tasks very clear at the outset. Give your brain good reason for being productive. Seduce it into coming up with the goods. 'Towards' motivators might include:

- Praise or glory for having completed the task.

- A tangible reward or treat.

- An earlier finishing time.

- The chance to move on to something more rewarding.

- Seeing a job through to the end.

- The benefit to a colleague or client.

- Money.

Possible 'away-from' motivators might include:

- Not staying late.

- No nagging from the boss.

- No angry clients.

- No more guilt.

- Fear about what might happen if it's not completed to deadline.

Most people quote 'money' as their greatest motivator in the workplace but you need to understand the limitations of hard cash in respect to task achievement. Money moves you, but it doesn't drive you. It can make us do what we don't want to do but it can't make us like the task. Would you tear six pages out of this book and eat them? You wouldn't choose to do this thing and you wouldn't want to. Yet I could move you to do it. How? By offering you money. You might do it for one pound or you might only be tempted by one million, but I could get you to do it at some price.

Money in the form of pay is compensation, not a motivator. It is provided to get you out of bed in the morning at an hour you would rather be sleeping and it is provided to ensure you stay in an office all day when you would, very likely, prefer to be at home or on a beach. Use money to self-motivate, but do so by *seeing* the things that money will help you acquire.

Mission statements

These are often used to motivate a workforce. Pinned to the wall they should turn lethargic into dynamic and wander into focus.

Mission statements fail for two reasons, though: they are either too non-specific or too long. If you are creating your own mission statement to galvanise your brain into action, keep it short and to the point. People will march for a sentence but not for a paragraph. Mission statements should be based in the future but most are rooted in present success. To most employees they are meaningless jargon. People only truly pay attention to what you *do*, not what you say. As a manager you may find time spent producing a mission statement is time wasted.

Motivate yourself towards intensity of focus by telling yourself both *why* you need to complete a certain task, and what the consequences will be if you don't get it right. Would you mind doing a job where a quarter of the day was spent washing your hands? You'd hate it, of course. But what if you were a surgeon? Surgeons understand the reason *why* they must spend so much time scrubbing up. They don't need monitoring. No one needs to check that they have done it. They understand implicitly *why* the hand washing is so vital. Turn your own attention on by giving it reasons to focus.

Thinking Rituals

I have touched on these but the technique is so important it merits redefining. You need to create:

1. Announcement gestures and rituals to get your brain going. These can be verbal commands or gestural wind-ups.

    Then you work through to:

2. Start-up rituals to psych yourself up, i.e. get into top gear.

    While you work you will need:

3. Thinking rituals to keep the pace and momentum going, followed by:

4. Announcements of ending – a formal agreement that you have stopped work for the time being.

1 Announcement rituals

These prepare the brain for high-focus activity. They will define your brain warm-up process to your subconscious, letting it know you mean business. The good thing is their simplicity. You probably do these anyway. The thing that makes them effective is their place in a ritual that is the same on each occasion. This builds recognition and obedience from your brain. It helps it to stop messing about and settle down to effort. Never break the ritual once it is started. Your subconscious should know that the process is non-negotiable. It can include:

◆ Having a coffee.

◆ Pacing.

◆ Tidying your desk.

◆ Cleaning your PC screen.

◆ Taking off or putting on your jacket.

◆ Closing any relaxation rituals down, i.e. closing a book firmly shut and putting it away in a drawer.

◆ Dabbing on an energising aromatherapy oil.

◆ Setting a timer.

◆ Using verbal prompts, like: Go! Go! Go!

2 Start-up rituals

Once you begin to gather speed these small rituals take you to the brink of performance, like:

◆ Banging palms of hands on desk.

◆ Writing the start and finish time across the top of your page.

◆ Verbal prompt: 'Focus and time-lock!

◆ Deep, noisy breath out and then in.

- Humming or whistling first bars of a tune you connect with energetic activity.

- Putting up a 'Do not disturb' notice, even if you are working alone.

NB: no unfinished business!

Never start work with an unfinished coffee or food. Never leave half-finished work nearby. Drink, eat and complete before you start or you will never reach peak performance. Use further snacks as a reward treat for when you have finished.

3 Thinking rituals

These keep you to the pace and speed you require for your brain to complete the task in the given time. These can include:

- Metronomic rituals, like tapping or rocking in your seat.

- Whistling under your breath.

- A ticking clock or timer.

- A short-term screensaver; you know you need to keep working to keep it off the screen.

- High-energy music in the background.

4 Announcements of ending

When you want to quit, quit. Shut down, don't rest or start something else as a gap-creator. Time your choreographed gap or tell yourself you have finished that job for the day. Use:

- Get out of programme or file on PC.

- Switch into screensaver.

- Get up and walk away.

- ◆ Go and get that coffee.

- ◆ Stretch.

- ◆ Close everything formally, including books and documents related to the task.

- ◆ Use a verbal affirmation. Announce out loud that you have finished.

CHAPTER TWO

Emotions Slow You Down

'Learn to repeat endlessly to yourself: it all
depends on me.'
ANDRÉ GIDE

— *Quick Tips* —————————————————

- ◆ When you are in a difficult transaction write down how you are feeling.

- ◆ Ask yourself: will these emotions help or hinder the process?

- ◆ If they will hinder, move them off the field of play.

- ◆ Work on your confidence and self-esteem.

- ◆ Avoid unnecessary conflict.

- ◆ Work on ways to keep business relationships flowing.

- ◆ Keep out of office politics.

- ◆ Never speak badly of people behind their back.

- ◆ Stop moaning and start doing.

- ◆ Solve problems, don't create them.

- ◆ Think of work as a place for great teamships, not great friendships.

Are you moody at work? If so, you are a prime Time Bandit, affecting both your colleagues' and your own work-effectiveness by dominating precious conscious thinking time with your own issues. Emotions can be either good or bad. All of them have value, because they prove we are human. The problem with emotions in the workplace is that they hijack the brain cells, causing attention deficiencies, and they scupper our strategies by clouding the issue when there is a problem.

For instance, how much time do you think you spend during the working day doing any of the following:

+ Seething
+ Resenting
+ Getting annoyed or angry
+ Worrying
+ Feeling embarrassed
+ Feeling upset
+ Feeling insecure
+ Feeling nervous
+ Planning revenge
+ Disliking colleagues
+ Getting involved with office politics
+ Moaning
+ Being shy
+ Lacking confidence
+ Annoying other people
+ Upsetting other people
+ Getting one over on other people
+ Competing
+ Envying
+ Taking things personally

The quickest way from A to B in the workplace is the calm, confident, coping route. Emotions create slowing mechanisms in the brain.

Keep in mind the eternal triangle of:

Feelings affecting
Thoughts affecting
Behaviour
(affecting feelings, affecting thoughts, etc.)

Negative feelings turn into non-useful behaviours.

Office Rage

Emotions can be one-dimensional, too. According to statistics, one in four of us have beaten up our computer, mainly in a rage against 'in-box tyranny'. Remember the way rock stars in the 1960s would throw TVs through hotel windows? Well, the trend is coming to an office near you. Only this decade it's more likely to be the frustrated office worker and his/her PC. The International Stress Management Association ranks e-mails among the top twenty causes of stress.

Office rage can be aimed at other mechanical workplace objects, such as a slow lift, a photocopier that breaks down or a coffee machine that delivers the wrong order. Colleagues can, of course, trigger attacks too. Small acts of rudeness or thoughtlessness can induce almost as much anger as more overt actions.

Rage is anger that has been badly channelled. The stress we suffer from the larger pressures, anxieties and challenges of the job may be bearable. After all, we go to work knowing we will be given tasks and deadlines. What makes that particular pressure cooker blow can be the smaller triggers. Things we know we shouldn't get worked up about. Like the muzak while we wait on hold on the phone, or the irritating background noise while we're talking to a client. The resulting emotion may seem disproportionate. In fact it's down to the transference factor: responding to one incident with emotions gleaned from another.

Emotional Control

So how can you stop your own emotions? Of course it isn't easy. Stopping them altogether would be unrealistic and even undesirable. What we need to learn to do is stop emotions affecting our efficiency and our time management. To do this you need to work on two key areas:

1. Building inner self-esteem. Confident people tend to be less emotionally damaged by external events.

2. Recognising and building the gap between the stimulus and the response.

What happens to us is not primarily responsible for the effect on our feelings and our behaviour. It is the way we process the stimulus that has that effect. Take the 'difficult' boss. He/she may leave staff feeling nervous, wary and demotivated. There is nearly always at least one member of the team who is unaffected by the boss's behaviour, though. To them it is water off a duck's back. They take it in their stride.

What frightens/upsets/angers one person can have the opposite effect on another. The stimulus is the same but it has been processed differently. You can't always control the stimulus. Things happen. But you always get the option of controlling your response.

Learn to change the script. Turn your negative energy, i.e. thoughts and words wasted on worrying or moaning, into positive or non-affected responses.

Logic Rules?

It is not true to say that logical thinkers get work done quicker. Left-brain activists tend to work in linear ways and sometimes their style can be too full of detail, checking and 'doing it by the book', to be speedy. Left-brainers don't care for rushing, hunches or jumping to conclusions. Their decisions are based on fact and research. They like reassurance that the idea has been tried and tested and not found wanting.

However, the left side of the brain is the side that most closely resembles a computer. Which means it can be nippy. If your computer wants to access stored information it can get there quickly, much faster than most humans. Why? Well, mainly because it doesn't have an emotional output. When you ask it the question it doesn't get anxious it may not know the answer. It doesn't worry about being taken for granted, or tell you to go and ask another PC because it wants to get home on time for a change.

Emotions are a barrier to time management in business. Often we waste time on over-think. We worry, we speculate, we seethe and we get hurt. We are fond of taking things personally. We believe most people to be working on a hidden agenda, so that, even if we are paid a compliment, we suspect something negative is behind it. If you set yourself or your team an objective you can bet emotions will provide your biggest barrier to achieving that objective. They scupper any strategy you can care to come up with.

Teams work best under crisis situations. Why? Because everyone is aware of the objective and no one allows emotions to get in the way. Ineffective teams have squabbles and spats. There are power-struggles and relationships break down. If there was an earthquake, though, even the worst team would get stuck in. Pecking orders and personality clashes would be forgotten while the task of rescue was being achieved. In other words, the emotional imbalance would move out of the picture.

Emotions blur clarity of purpose. They create subobjectives that appear more crucial than your prime objective. When we are motivated by anger or revenge, rather than reason, we will often take the wrong route. Emotion in business wastes too many valuable brain cells. We spend too long worrying about what might happen in the future and chewing over what has already happened in the past, and not enough time taking care of the here and now.

Take control. There is one company I work for that seems to wind me up the moment I walk through the door. However much

I tell myself to stay calm and laugh it off, I can never get as far as the lift without beginning to suffer the first twinges of frustration and annoyance. This means my head is not clear for the work I have to do.

My mood affects my effectiveness, though. It's hard to think with all that emotion stirred up in my head. We need to off-load.

When you are planning any effective, time-economic strategy, start by writing down your overall goal/s. Then ask yourself: how do I feel about this person/meeting/situation? If you are ringing a client to get business you may feel awkward. If you are handling a complaint you may feel lacking in confidence. If you have to criticise someone's work you may feel embarrassed. If you have to give a keynote business presentation you may feel nervous.

The next question to ask is: will those feelings help or hinder this transaction? The answer will be obvious. They will hinder. You need logic, calm and reason to create the best strategy. You need the left side of your brain.

Left-side Thinking

Learn to turn this side of the brain on and off. By tapping into it you will be in control of a situation, rather than letting the situation control you. It is responsible for:

- Analytical functions
- Verbal skills
- Rational thinking
- Order
- Numeracy

Right-side Thinking

If you allow this side to run amok, you will be reacting, rather than responding to situations. Which means the situations will control you, rather than the other way around. You will be less in control of yourself. It is responsible for:

* Artistic ability
* Creativity
* Visual and spatial ability
* Intuition
* Synthetic reasoning

Primary and Secondary Emotions

Most of our emotional responses in the workplace are secondary. Primary emotions are the more primitive responses to threatening situations. Their main function is to allow us to survive. Secondary emotions are the ones produced by thoughts or the imagination. Each type of emotion has a physiological, a behavioural and a subjective effect.

You think about a colleague who has annoyed you. Your heart rate increases as you revisit that anger. Your face reddens. Your muscles tense. You respond by bashing off a rude e-mail or moaning about them to someone at the next desk. Because they have been triggered by emotion, these responses tend to be reactive, rather than responsive, and are therefore rarely useful long term. Their main aim is to make you emotionally satisfied. Shouting at someone who has made you angry will create a moment of emotional satisfaction. This will dissolve, though, when you begin to feel guilty or ashamed of your lack of control, or upset by the victim's response.

Or you might transfer that anger to another situation, getting irritated with someone else over something petty and shouting at them, instead. Or you may even take that anger home with you and blast off at your partner or children.

Masking

Emotions in business are famously unpopular. Like the Japanese, the British corporate culture tends towards the belief that to show unmasked emotion is to somehow lose face. It is a sign that you are not in control of yourself. In client situations it is a complete liability.

So we indulge in what is known as 'masking': covering up our true negative feelings with a display of politeness or, at worst, indifference. We smile when we are told we've lost that contract. We act calm in the face of aggression. We look interested when we are bored. We 'sit' on our emotions to be professional. The trouble is, this often means they brew up inside, resulting in ineffective thinking and stress. Both of these become a time-management issue. You can't work well if you are seething or upset. Your brain can't focus on the job in hand.

People in emotional jobs, like medical workers, carers and the police, have to learn how to control their emotional responses. A carer can only be of help to their victim if they can keep a cool head and act professionally.

Steps for Dealing With Your Emotions

1. Write down how you are feeling. This will help you to be more analytical.

2. Allow yourself to have emotions in the workplace; after all, you are human. Learn how to move them off the field of play while the game is going, though.

3. Use positive affirmations to talk yourself round. Tell yourself you are feeling calm, serene, happy, unworried . . . whatever. Then repeat, repeat, repeat. Or repeat: 'Life's too short . . . Life's too short . . .'

4. Never get into a fight with pigs; you'll get all dirty and they'll just enjoy it.

5. Take a moment. When a situation begins to make you emotional, walk away, if possible. Pause. Breathe out. Get back in control of yourself and the situation.

6. Stop yourself crying. Whatever it takes, stem the flow. Tears tend to be self-perpetuating. A couple would be OK but once you start you can't stop. Proper blubbing is embarrassing because you lose control. Embarrassment and/or self-pity make us cry harder. Look up at the ceiling and stop blinking for a few seconds to make the eyes dry. Stare up at the light. Press a tissue beneath your lower lashes to soak up any sign of tears. Press a fingernail into the palm of your hand.

7. Try not to discuss your feelings with colleagues. This tends to make them grow, rather than diminish.

8. Exercise your way out of a temper. Run on the spot. Walk up and down stairs. Go for a fast walk around the block. Tense and flex every muscle in your body.

9. Splash cold water on to your face.

10. Go somewhere private and pace around, telling yourself off out loud. Watch the tennis stars at Wimbledon talk to themselves out loud to get back in control when they're losing. Do the same. Pace and rant. Pause. Breathe out all the negative emotion. Pull yourself up. Pull a serene face. Then smile. You're back in control.

11. Stop thinking you are perfect. Admit mistakes. Learn to take criticism. Roll with the punches. Resentment and anger often stem out of a desire to repair self-esteem following criticism or disagreement. True confidence means you are open-minded to genuine critics but unharmed by slights.

12. Tell the person how you feel, but without acting out the emotion. You could say: 'I feel very angry about what you just did', but do it without shouting or banging about.

13. Write it all in your Little Book of Madness, your personal, carry-everywhere log of negative feelings.

14. Laugh, instead. The act of smiling contracts the facial muscles, which decreases the blood flow, which lowers the temperature of the brain stem. This lowers the levels of serotonin, which makes you feel better.

Hot Tips for Improved Networking and Self-marketing

Update your skills

◆ Prioritise some training time. Updating your IT skills, especially, is invested time.

◆ Use e-learning to fast-track your training.

◆ Some universities even offer an on-line MBA, so you can study anywhere, anytime.

◆ More than 20 per cent of training is expected to be on-line within the next five years.

◆ Research courses via the net on: www.floodlight.co.uk, www.hotcourses.com, www.learndirect.co.uk, and the Open University at www.open.ac.uk.

Accept your mistakes

◆ Recognise your own mistakes as soon as possible. Don't bluff yourself. Know when you are wrong and don't be stubborn about it.

◆ Consider confessing. Speed up the repair process.

◆ Avoid too much 'kitty-littering'. This is covering up small mistakes until they begin to create a big stink.

Be pro-active

◆ Set personal long- and short-term goals.

◆ Think 'solutions' as well as 'problems'. Use the word 'there-fore' after each barrier pops up in your mind, as in: 'I have a problem with space in my office, there's nowhere to put any-thing which means my desk is chaotic . . . therefore . . . I need to ask for a larger office/get a better filing system/move things out of the way.'

◆ Dress smart. *American Corporate Trends* magazine polled a 50 per cent drop in commitment to the job, a 35 per cent rise in lateness and a 63 per cent increase in customer complaints on dress-down Fridays.

◆ Reclaim your weekend. According to surveys we work the longest hours in Europe, with a 60-hour-plus week being the norm for one in nine workers. Weekend working makes you less efficient, as you cut down time spent on vital relaxation. About half of us are often too tired to have sex.

◆ If weekend work is an organisational expectation, consider approaching your boss about a change in culture. Tell him or her that a weekend break pays dividends to the company as well as the employee, in terms of increased productivity, energy and staff retention.

◆ Keep three plastic bricks on your desk, one green, one yellow and one red. Place the green one out when you are available to talk, the yellow one when you are working but able to be interrupted if necessary and the red one when you are working and don't want to be disturbed. Tell colleagues what the colours mean and add some buy-in for them, i.e.: 'It will save you having to hang about until I've finished.' Encourage them to use the same or a similar system. If you are a manager, supply the bricks for your team. Make sure you use them effectively. Never leave the red one there when you are available, or others will begin to distrust the system and interrupt you to ask.

◆ Never eat at your desk.

Organise your networking

◆ Network with other departments. Take time to go and introduce yourself. This will raise your profile, to fast-track promotion or sideways moves. It also helps to speed up communication. People communicate more effectively if they have met face to face.

◆ If there is a regular glitch with yourself and another department, go and speak to them face to face. Tell them about the problem and ask what you can both do to solve it. Don't get into conflict and don't try to apportion blame, it only slows the process up.

◆ When you are networking at business/social events, work quickly and effectively. Get round to the maximum amount of clients without appearing to rush. Eight to ten per hour is a good average. Plan beforehand. Know some good openers (nothing too clever, 'What do you do?' or 'How are things in your company?' will do, as long as you remember to sound interested in the answer). Build your next comment around the answer and know the objective of the gathering (i.e., to talk business, sell a new product or just to socialise).

◆ Know how to get away to mingle, or you will get held up. Take your guest and introduce him/her to someone else.

Getting it all together

◆ Have a debrief immediately after the event. Staff may be tired but it is the best time to find out what was said and what needs to be followed up. Debrief quickly but thoroughly, taking notes and delegating follow-up action on the spot. Get others to make a note of individual actions, too. Never assume you'll remember things in the morning.

♦ Never get left with that cluster of 'now who was that?' business cards in your pocket. When you are given a card, wait until you are out of sight and write necessary details or action on the back of it, e.g. phone for a meeting about marketing ideas' or 'could be hot date', etc.

♦ Put a finish time as well as a start time for your event on the invites. This is perfectly acceptable socially and it gives guests an idea when to order cabs.

♦ Fast-track friendships are vital in building business relationships with clients. Create instant rapport by mirroring, i.e. slightly copying the client's body-language style. Do the same with vocal tone and jargon.

♦ Keep a file on your clients, noting personal details as well as business information. If they tell you they have a Ferrari or three kids at university it allows you to open the conversation at the place you left off, even if you only meet every six months. This also allows you to appear hugely charming and charismatic as they will think you have remembered details about them. Avoid getting too clever, though, or you could begin to sound creepy.

♦ Use your business small talk to discover mutual interests. I found one client hard going until we discovered we both lived in Islington and then it became hard to shut the conversation down.

♦ If the small talk does become time-consuming, feel free to steer the conversation back to business. Be polite but firm and make some comment of regret, to show you were enjoying the chit-chat.

♦ Use closed questions when you need to extract information quickly.

Using a meeting effectively

◆ When you go to a client meeting, do as much homework on the account and the company beforehand as possible. Display some of this knowledge at the meeting and you may save a lengthy induction from the client. I find hours pass listening to 'The history and structure of our company' monologues otherwise.

◆ When you are at a client meeting do as much on-the-spot work as possible, to avoid future delay. If you need to get a figure or check something get your mobile out and do it quickly there and then.

◆ Warn colleagues that you are on a key client visit and might be phoning in for details or research. Get them to help fast-track your connection.

Efficient client liaison

◆ Build your client relationships around the 'diamond' structure. Most are built around the 'bow-tie', where the sole connection between a company and its suppliers is between the buyer and the account manager. This leads to lengthy, time-consuming communications, where one contacts the other (usually with difficulty) and they then pass messages or orders on internally. In a 'diamond' structure the account manager and buyer stand at the outer two points. The main hub of the business is done direct between the compatible departments of the companies.

◆ Keep a complete and up-to-date log of every account, including its movements and the people dealing with it. Call this up on screen, just in case, every time you need to speak to the client.

◆ Always avoid wasting time logging on mid-call by pulling up statistics before you pick up the phone. If a client calls you, get the data on screen as you go through your small talk.

◆ Keep a record of client interests and small talk details. Know when they are due to give birth or get married. Know that they have just bought a boat or a house in the Algarve. Pick the conversation up again seamlessly, even if there is a gap of several months between meetings.

And finally

◆ No time to get to the gym? Exercise at your desk. Read *Rosie's Armchair Exercises* by Rosita Evans, Discovery Books.

CHAPTER THREE

Office Politics

'Bloody noses are great teachers.'
JOSEPH McKINNEY

Quick Tips

♦ Do you: bitch, manipulate, blame, pass the buck, gossip, brown-nose, plot, scheme and lie? If so, you indulge in office politics.

♦ Stop it.

♦ Stop encouraging others.

♦ Become honest, fair and assertive.

♦ Create goals and define teams.

In the modern business landscape office politics lie as a quaint, ancient paradox. We work with computers, dealing with facts and logic. And yet we still carefully pull one another apart on a regular basis. The craft of office politics is both ancient and lethal. When we work, we work in tribes, rather than teams. We operate as individuals within the scope of group goals or 'visions'. We work together because that way we know we are stronger and yet we frequently fight just as fiercely within our own pack as we do with our rivals.

Some companies manage to present a civilised, united front. Others seethe with political skulduggery. Groups form within the pack and set about competing with other factions. There are leaders and would-be leaders and natural leaders who are forced to follow, and natural followers who are forced to lead. There are bosses squabbling over support staff and sales teams squabbling over targets. We are human, therefore we squabble. It is the way of the world. Self-interest is invariably at the heart of it but then who isn't interested in themselves?

If you think all this battling is time-consuming you'd be right. It's like trying to complete a marathon while simultaneously chewing off your own leg. It doesn't work. It slows you down and it wears you out and it can slow you down to the point of stopping. It upsets you and makes you feel insecure. It can be stressful. It needs to be managed. But to manage it effectively would be to fight evolution.

The pack squabbles to stay alive. It needs a pecking order and that will always be challenged. The fact that the squabbling becomes self-destructive is almost irrelevant.

Office Gossip

Recent research has it that gossiping originated in the Stone Age and that women used it as a key weapon. Whether that sounds likely or not, now that men have discovered an enthusiasm for the genre it has become the most effective method of business communication. The grapevine may be speedy, then, but unfortunately it is time counter-productive in terms of business productivity.

How to Avoid Office Politics

With no wish to sound negative, this is going to be a tough call, especially if your workplace is no stranger to intrigue. The big problem with politics is that it always manages to be someone else's fault. We are all sociable, fair-minded people and it's only the other lot that ruin things by being malicious and backbiting. With that thought in mind, here are some tips to stay clear of the pack:

◆ Imagine the impossible: what if it is *you* who is starting the scraps? Think long and hard before answering truthfully.

◆ When you start a new job be polite to everyone but wait before starting up friendships. See how the land lies. Discover what the packs look like. Keep a sociable distance until you know it is safe.

◆ Avoid spreading gossip.

◆ Avoid speaking ill of anyone.

◆ Try not to agree when someone else speaks ill of someone.

◆ Be assertive. Communicate as openly and honestly as possible. Don't sit on problems and start seething. But be tactful, too.

◆ Don't join in – put yourself in the role of impartial observer.

◆ Think team dynamics as well as personal glory.

◆ Be a bad audience for backbiting. Keep quiet and lower your eyes to register disinterest.

◆ If someone at work irritates or angers you, refuse to take it personally. Remind yourself that life is too short to get strung out over the small stuff.

◆ Respond, don't react.

◆ Never sweat the small stuff.

Getting Buy-in From Your Colleagues

This does not mean you have to win a popularity contest. Getting your team to function effectively without the time-consuming distractions of in-fighting and backstabbing will mean your communication and persuasion skills need to be honed to the point of perfection. Teams will unite under a banner of a comprehensive goal. When you explain your goals you need to do more than just 'tell', though.

According to leading business consultant Steve Prince, when you tell someone something you give information. This is not the same thing as communicating. 'Telling,' says Steve, 'is like showing someone your holiday snaps. The pictures mean something to you because you had the entire experience. They are a point of reference that helps you relive smells, tastes, sights and feelings. To the other viewer they are just plain dull. They represent something that is outside their experience.'

Motivating and persuading others, creating buy-in, requires you to get the others to see, feel and smell the outcome of your vision, too. To do this you must also work to their values, rather than your own. Go back to the holiday story. To engage someone in your otherwise boring tale you would relate the parts of your experience that they would find interesting. If someone is a foodie you might describe a mouth-watering meal. If someone else is an artist you could describe the views. I would only come awake when the fashion shopping was mentioned. We all have different tastes and desires. Play to those of your colleagues if you want to get them onside.

If the politics are part of the culture you may need to get into some choreographed open discussion. Resentments run deep, but if people have a 'gloves-off' opportunity to speak what has been festering in their mind – with a facilitator keeping an eye out for signs of conflict – they may be given a chance to heal. A lot of resentment is based on misunderstandings. Allowing people a chance to explain their motives can help. These meetings can include any number, but everyone should take a pledge to do the following:

◆ Talk openly, honestly and with integrity.

◆ Listen with an open mind.

◆ Leave emotions out of the meeting.

◆ Change some agreed aspect of their behaviour.

◆ Commit to specific, measurable steps to go forward once agreements have been reached.

Defusing Conflict

◆ Keep a cool head.

◆ Repeat: 'I feel calm, confident and in control'.

◆ Respond, don't react.

◆ Create a gap between the stimulus and the response. Move away, if necessary.

◆ Reflect back the other person's main points.

◆ Avoid 'rage' words, like 'should', 'can't', 'as I've already said', 'so what you're trying to say is . . .', 'whatever', 'if you say so', etc.

◆ Negotiate adult to adult.

◆ Look for any common ground.

◆ Listen.

◆ Be flexible.

◆ Respect the other person's right to have a view.

◆ Don't negate their feelings about something.

- Stick to what's relevant.

- Stick to the issue under discussion.

- Work towards a compromise.

- Work towards a functional relationship. The issue isn't friendship.

- Treat every member of the team as valuable.

- Look for solutions, not blame or recrimination.

- Jettison past baggage if it proves unhelpful. Drop old gripes.

- Start with a friendly gesture to break the ice. Bring coffee or muffins.

- Listen to their problems first and make an offer to change or help the situation.

- Don't be defensive about complaints.

- Don't argue about complaints.

- Take at least one immediate step towards getting a solution.

Selling the Goals

Nothing is more exhausting than working with a team that you have to drag towards your goals. One colleague who has been organising an important conference referred to the experience of dealing with her company's staff as like swimming through porridge. The venue booking was easy and so was getting the big-name speakers to attend. But things began to collapse when she tried to motivate the staff who were going to market the tickets and assist in the running. She received no support, which led to conflict. Worse still, those who promised to help let her down at the last minute.

She has been given the task of organising a similar event every year. Since then she has picked her brains to work out how to motivate the group. She has come up with the following suggestions:

◆ Include some of the key staff at an earlier stage.

◆ Inspire them with the vision of the conference. Tell them stories about how good it will be.

◆ Get them more involved with the famous-name speakers.

◆ Brief them regularly to build up some air of excitement.

◆ Tell them the outcome if any of the tasks they agree to undertake go wrong.

◆ Ask their opinions. Allow them some input and a degree of control and responsibility.

◆ Brief and debrief.

◆ Sew in a couple of perks along the way.

◆ Buy them a drink when it's over.

Active Change

If a situation or relationship isn't working then something needs to change. Behaviour breeds behaviour. Is your behaviour negative as a result of negative stimuli? Or did you activate that negativity? Either way it might be you who has to make the change in tactics or behaviour to find a solution. You may not be able to influence or make the other person or people change, in which case it has to be down to you.

Be analytical about the transaction. Think in terms of adult/child/parent behaviour patterns. Who is being the child? Who is being the logical, fair-minded adult who wants to find a solution? Most of us can uncover something of the child in our own response, e.g. sulking, stubbornness, passivity, aggression, resentment, etc. Scrutinise your own approach. Where is the opportunity to make a shift? Work towards breaking the deadlock. Don't think of it in terms of 'backing down' or 'losing face'. Compare it to the tactics a parent would use on a difficult child. What might cause a breakthrough?

If you feel yourself getting bogged down in the negative aspects of office politics, think of the value of working in a pack or team:

♦ You can pool ideas and resources.

♦ You can discuss problems and solutions.

♦ You can produce results faster and more efficiently when you all work together.

♦ If you have six members of a team you have six times the brain capacity and potential for ideas.

♦ You don't get lonely.

♦ You are stronger against an enemy.

Proactive or Reactive?

Take a long look at your approach to your life. Are you proactive or reactive?

Proactive

♦ Confident
♦ In control
♦ Optimistic
♦ Problem solving
♦ Assertive
♦ Able to change
♦ Perceived as lucky

Reactive

* Let things happen to you
* Controlled by events
* Worry
* Unable to speak your mind
* Fight or flight when under pressure
* In a state of 'learned helplessness', i.e. in the mindset that whatever you do it won't make a difference

It's the reactive people who indulge in office politics. Lacking confidence in their own abilities they decide to fight dirty. In doing so they destroy team dynamics. The office becomes a place where everything is sweated but nothing gets done because people are too busy watching their backs. This is a time issue. To become proactive:

◆ Get to know people and what makes them tick.

◆ Listen, don't assume.

◆ Check five times before fighting back.

◆ Try the open negotiation and discussion route before playing dirty.

◆ Never retaliate like with like.

◆ Revenge is rarely sweet. Look at your overall goals.

◆ Never be a doormat if people attack you. Tell them about behaviours you want changing, or that you find intolerable. Move towards a solution, rather than harbouring resentment.

◆ Learn to cope if they won't change. Change your response.

◆ Keep in dialogue, even if it is difficult. Avoidance and silence are two of the most destructive weapons in business.

◆ Be calm but never patronise.

◆ Keep topping up the self-esteem.

CHAPTER FOUR

Home Working

Office working is rapidly changing, as the following shows:

◆ The number of managers working a six-day week has fallen from one in five in 1998 to one in ten today.

◆ Three out of four managers said their workload has increased in the past three years.

◆ The demand for flexible working and home working is increasing but few companies are restructuring sufficiently to meet it.

You might start thinking about reclaiming your life.

Quick Tips

◆ Be clear that the culture is for you before volunteering.

◆ Decide which work is appropriate for home work and which suits an office environment.

◆ Maintain a dialogue with colleagues.

◆ Only e-mail the speedy stuff. Use human contact as well.

◆ Prioritise your workload.

◆ Avoid distractions, like cleaning, chores and breakfast TV.

◆ Set time targets and deadlines, just as you would in the office.

Starting From Home

Home working should be the ultimate salvation for the terminally time-consumed. Take all those Time Bandits out of your day, like office gossips, meetings, on-call emergencies and commuting, and what have you got? A day of intensive, productive work without distraction or interruption. A day where every hour equals three of office time. A haven of uninterrupted comfort.

And so it is – for at least the first couple of weeks.

Time Bandits pop up everywhere, though. There are probably more than you thought in your own house.

Displacement Activities

These will be your greatest barrier to making your home working time-efficient. There are always distractions in the office. You put off your main tasks by chatting, making phone calls and doodling through your PC.

At home, though, there are a million more potential displacement activities. These range from the mundane, like dusting or restacking your CD collection in alphabetical order, to more crucial tasks like repaving the patio or running a neighbour's kid to the hospital.

Deciding on Home Working

Perhaps you are currently deciding whether home working is for you or not. Maybe, like a lot of firms, yours is giving you the option to spend a part of your week working long-distance. If other members of staff have already gone down this route you may have already felt the pangs of envy when you phone them and hear birdsong or crackling log fires in the background. For some reason home workers always sound as though they are lying in a hammock sipping a Pimms.

Before you decide to do home working answer the following few questions:

1. What do you enjoy most in your current job?

2. Would those factors still occur if you worked from home?

3. How much time per week do you currently spend commuting?

4. How much time do you currently spend fire-fighting, i.e. tackling small crises that break out that would be someone else's panic if you were not available at your desk?

5. How much of a 'people' person are you? Do you like to work with others as part of a team?

6. Do you prefer working alone, in a quiet atmosphere?

7. Is your home atmosphere quiet?

8. Are you likely to end up fire-fighting at home, i.e. dealing with small crises that would not bother you if you weren't available?

9. Do you currently use your home as a haven away from work?

10. How do you think you would cope with the intrusion if your home became your office, too?

11. Do you have a space at home that you are willing to donate?

12. Are the rest of the family happy about that use of the space?

13. How many other family members will be home during the day?

14. Are you better at face-to-face or telephone communication?

15. Do you want to home work full-time or just one day per week?

Then weigh up the pros and cons:

Pros

◆ No commuting, which means less hassle and more hours in the working day.

◆ No background noise.

◆ Healthier environment – less pollution, more fresh air, more natural light, less germs from others.

◆ No interruptions.

◆ Less emotional hassle via office politics.

◆ Fewer wardrobe decisions.

◆ No machine coffee.

◆ Cheaper and healthier food.

◆ More breaks.

◆ Better places to go during those breaks.

◆ Control of incoming communication.

◆ Control of room temperature.

◆ Choice of music or silence.

◆ More time spent with your family, pets, neighbours, etc.

◆ Working to body clock, rather than the one on the wall.

Cons

◆ Harder to get out of bed with no train to catch.

◆ More hours may mean extra jobs instead, like the school run or shopping for food.

◆ You may find the silence difficult if you have become used to working with noise. Or you might have a noisy house, especially during school holidays.

- The healthy aspect of your home environment depends entirely on your habits when you work alone. For instance, you may smoke, which was banned in the office, drink booze at odd times, eat too much and put on weight, sit badly because no one is watching, etc.

- It is a complete myth that there are fewer interruptions at home. People pop in. Pets climb over your PC and sit on the keyboard, daytime TV becomes like a magnet, the doorbell rings more times than you have ever imagined, plants call out to be watered.

- Colleagues still ring to keep you up to speed with the gossip.

- You might miss dressing up.

- Hot drinks take longer to make. You'll miss Starbucks.

- Constant grazing for food can lead to massive weight gain.

- More breaks mean more nibbling.

- You need to be assertive with people. Family members start asking you to do chores while you're 'off'. Friends ring. Parents offer to visit. Neighbours pop in for coffee.

- Your body clock might be excessively lazy.

- You can get bored.

- You will get lonely.

- You may find you feel old, as though you've already retired. Most of the other people you see walking about may be elderly or with kids. You'll start noticing the Saga ads on TV.

Time Flies When You're Having Fun

You will be amazed how many things vie for your time when you're working from home. This morning alone I have been waylaid from writing this chapter by several non-negotiable emergencies; here are five of them:

1. The need to watch the man collect the recycling bins.

2. The need to stare at a car parked outside my house and wonder if it is dumped.

3. The need to read three newspapers and the weekend colour supplements.

4. The need to dust.

5. The need to tidy my knicker drawer.

Rules of Engagement

To make home working time cost-effective you will need to be even more disciplined than you were in the workplace. House rules should include:

Getting started

♦ A set time for getting out of bed. Stuff all that body clock nonsense, your brain and responses will do as you tell them. Instruct yourself to wake at the same time every day. Leave it to chance and you may find yourself rousing later and later but still feeling as tired. Wake-up time needs to be non-negotiable.

♦ Get dressed. Sounds obvious? Yet a lot of home workers find it incredibly easy to be discovered by returning family still clad in slippers and dressing gown at 6.00 pm.

♦ Never watch breakfast TV. It's like soft drugs are to hard drugs. Never think you can play with it but still keep in control. One day you'll find *Kilroy* is on and then it's downhill through to *Neighbours*. Don't switch on. Switching on is easy. Switching off is a completely different ball game.

Developing some good habits

♦ Keep a few rituals in the day.

♦ Go to a gym. If you can afford the membership visit at 7.00 am before you start work. You'll feel far more virtuous and your brain will be buzzing. Plus you may be less likely to pile on the kilos.

♦ Make a rule of 'home equals healthy'. Don't smoke there. Fill the fridge with bottled water and organic snacks. Break for stretching exercises. Condition your hair. Use a face mask.

♦ Think ergonomics. Your chair should be comfortable and support your back. Your desk needs to be the right height. Invest in the proper stuff, if you can. Perhaps your company will fund you. Sitting on the kitchen chair with one leg tucked under the other will cause long-term damage.

♦ Work with nice soft light; you will get more choice at home.

♦ Talk to yourself. It keeps the vocal chords warmed up for any client phone calls, and keeps the brain working in 'clear verbal communication mode'. When I have been tucked away writing a novel I find I am struggling to communicate with even close friends because my brain has been set on 'think' rather than 'speak' mode.

♦ Set times in the day to do any seemingly vital home chores, like cleaning.

♦ Make set times for 'reward slots'. All the nice things you can do at home, like eating ice cream and phoning a friend, should only be done as a reward for some work. Get into the cult of delayed gratification. Home workers become instant gratification merchants. This doesn't work. Be your own strict boss.

Keeping in touch

◆ If you work from home more than one day a week you may find a sense of bereavement as you start to get out of touch with office culture. Phone in regularly to be kept up to speed.

◆ Make your own end of the line sound professional. *Never* let the kids answer the business line, or – horror of horrors – record your answer machine message. This isn't cute, it's ghastly. Keep marauding pets out of the way, too. Ringing your home shouldn't sound like you're interrupting a busy episode of *The Waltons*.

◆ If you work in the garden (and why not) find some way of muffling the sounds. People will assume you're skiving.

◆ Get your company to install a business line. Put an answering machine on the other so that you don't get interrupted by social calls while you work. This also means you don't find yourself taking business calls after office hours.

Being organised

◆ The good thing about home working is that your timekeeping can be noisier. Buy a kitchen timer for your desk and set it each time you allot a deadline for a job.

◆ Keep a tidy ship. Even though no one sees your desk you'll need to keep it clear of clutter. Clear up each night before allowing yourself to quit for the day.

◆ A crucial point of the home working day is start-up. Learn to 'double-bag' your morning chores so that they include something that means you're geared up for business. I switch on my PC before I go down to the kitchen to make tea, so that I know it will be up and running by the time I get into my office. Always know what your first three office jobs of the day will be. Select things that are short, sharp and easily accomplished. They will act as your warm-up for the rest of the day.

♦ Compile a to-do list, exactly the way you would have done in the office. Make a separate one for household chores. Don't mix and match the two lists. Pick strictly from the business list during work hours and the household chores during breaks or out of hours. Combining the two could be your worst time-management mistake.

If you only intend working from home one day a week, work out the best use of your time there. Avoid doing stuff that you could have done better in the office. Candidates for home working include:

♦ Uninterrupted phone calls. Make a list of the calls you need to make and work your way through it. When you work from home you can often contact people at the times of the day that they are more likely to be available, like first thing, before 9.00 am.

♦ Creative thinking. Creativity dries up in a busy office environment. Use your time at home to flex the right side of your brain.

♦ Intense left-brain work. If you need peace and quiet to write proposals, work on figures, do some research or plan a written report, then this could be done from home.

Candidates for office-based work include:

♦ Anything that requires team-working.

♦ Meetings. I know these can be done as teleconferencing, but sometimes you just have to be face to face.

♦ Jobs where you need to give lots of instructions to admin.

♦ Selling.

♦ Persuading or influencing.

♦ Marketing yourself. A sad fact of home working is that you can become one of the lost tribe of employees if you aren't careful. Raising your profile is a vital part of long-term business success. Colleagues who attend the office each day may end up streets ahead in terms of promotional prospects and networking.

Procrastination: Hot Tips

'If a thing's hard to do then it's probably not worth doing.'
HOMER SIMPSON

◆ Be aware that you are guilty of putting things off. If you lie and make *excuses* to yourself, you'll never overcome the problem.

◆ Work in bite-size chunks. Create small deadlines within large ones.

◆ Work out why you're putting a job off. Is it down to: fear? Boredom? Dislike? Feeling overwhelmed? Laziness? Stress? Lack of enough information or equipment to achieve the task? Deal with these problems first.

◆ Create a reward for finishing, or a punishment for not.

◆ Tell yourself you are a starter *and* a finisher.

◆ Start with a ten-minute, high-focus, high-energy burst of effort. Everyone can manage ten minutes.

CHAPTER FIVE

Stress

'There are moments when everything goes well;
don't be frightened, it won't last.'
JULES RENARD

┌─ **Quick Tips** ──────────────────────────────┐

◆ Be aware of your stress levels.

◆ Monitor the highs and the lows.

◆ Work out where your ideal level of stimulation lies.

◆ Work out the stress 'triggers'.

◆ Take breaks.

◆ Keep working on your perception. Work is rarely
  life-threatening. Don't act as if it is.

◆ Create fun.

└───┘

Not only is stress a big Time Bandit, but it is also a very cunning
and manipulative one, too. Stress tends to make you feel you're
coping when you're not. It can make you busy to the point of
exhaustion, but without achievement of any goal. Stress makes
your efforts about as productive as a hamster on a wheel. You're
rotating faster and faster but you aren't getting anywhere.

The TUC considers stress the UK's top workplace hazard. Two-thirds of the companies they surveyed in 2000 considered stress a severe problem.

Points to remember about stress:

♦ It makes you stupid.

♦ It makes you emotionally unstable.

♦ It makes you unwell.

I think you can begin to see the challenge of stress in your time-management discipline.

Why Stupid?

Well, you know those moments when your brain is at its most effective? Usually they come when you're relaxing somewhere, like in the bath or in bed. One minute you're feeling drowsy and the next you discover Fermat's Last Theorem or you finally remember your granny's recipe for mayonnaise. Sadly you then nod off and forget it. I had a brain-clearing moment on an Intercity express the other day. Normally I read during long journeys, just to stop getting bored. The stuff I end up reading is usually eye-candy, like any celebrity magazine I can grab from the station. This creates non-productive time that I consider to be restful. This trip I romped through *Hello!* And ran out of reading matter. First I panicked then I tried to sleep. Finally I stared at the view. As a Londoner, though, there is a limit to the fascination value of grass, hedges and cows. Suddenly, though, my brain cleared. Good ideas started to float up through the ether. I got quotes for my book. I finally thought of the vital first line for a business talk I was giving, and it was *hilarious*. I formed a plot line for my next novel. Dead brain cells had suddenly become fertile again. It was as though someone had turned on the creative tap.

I pulled out a pen and scribbled everything down on the back of a hotel bill. When I got back to my office the next day I pulled it out and read it and – guess what? It was all solid gold. (You thought I was going to tell you it was gibberish.) I used the lot. It taught me how infrequently I remember to use my brain properly. I stopped squeezing it for a few minutes and it came up with the goods. Take the pressure off and thought clarity is the result. Ten minutes invested in brain rest is worth up to two hours of wine-press thinking.

Now what about those moments when your brain turns stupid on you? When you manage to forget your house number and you make some idiot mistake like trying to turn the baby off with the TV remote when it won't stop crying. These kinds of mistakes are made under pressure, or during periods of anxiety. The periods may be fleeting. A student may forget all he/she has studied during a crucial exam, but the knowledge will return once the end bell has gone.

The brain has ways of coping with crises. One way is to shut down the intellectual function and boot up the survival style of thinking. Your brain will rev up faster and faster but only to produce the sort of life-saving decisions you would need in an emergency. This is less than useless if your emergency involves delivering a sales presentation or attending a job interview. It's like Rambo turning up in place of Stephen Hawking.

Why Emotionally Unstable?

Think crisis situations again. Stress exaggerates the emotions. It is especially good at producing tears for no apparent reason, and anger and irritability. What you can't expect under stress is logic, reason, team-working and objective-led behaviour. Global objectives can go to hell when you're stressed. All your brain wants to tackle are non-useful issues like getting revenge and feeling resentment.

Why Unwell?

Not content with making you stupid and tearful, stress has a nice little party piece called 'breaking down your immune system' up its sleeve as well. So you get any illness that seems to be about, or recurring bouts of anything you normally suffer from occasionally. Stress can also bring its own set of symptoms with it. These will vary from person to person, but the most common will include:

* Headaches and migraine
* Backache
* Indigestion
* Palpitations
* Dizziness
* Hyperventilation
* Sweating
* Shaking
* Diarrhoea

Who's to Blame?

Don't make stress the main troublemaker, though. It was probably time – or lack of it – that caused it in the first place. In business the stress build-up usually goes something like this:

Task + deadline + constraints – support = pressure, which may in turn lead to stress.

This formula is not inevitable, though. We all expect to be given the task, after all that's what work is all about. We may enjoy the challenge of a deadline. It adds that little adrenaline hit that we need to rev us up into action. It's when those deadlines become unrealistic, either through workload or our own incompetence, and it's when things conspire to prevent us achieving them and it's when support is actively lacking that we start to turn feral.

Even with all that, though, it's possible to cope with and even enjoy some pressure. What needs to be added to the mix is *perception*. You need to care. You need to give a damn to get stressed. You need to *allow* things to get on top of you. Without your permission they just can't. How often do you lie down on the floor and allow life to use you as a doormat. How often do you accept the roles of 'upset', 'anxious', 'angered' or 'resentful' without question?

Change

We live in a culture of constant change in the workplace. This is often blamed for the high stress levels in some firms. Stress-causing change can be cultural, like the IT revolution and associated change in work practices, or it can be corporate, when firms merge or go through buy-outs.

It is a myth that change is bad. Change is necessary. Everything changes, but at different rates. Change may make you step outside your comfort zone but even that can be an uplifting experience. Even the oldest dogs can learn new tricks.

Change need not be stressful. Apart from *perception*, the other key word that links with stress is *control*. To create a climate that will breed stress you need to make people think they lack control in their lives and tasks.

It is easy for bosses to lead staff through change without producing a stress response. Just make sure you:

Inform

and

Consult

Most firms find it easier to leave employees in the dark, though. This means they have to resort to guesswork and rumour. And you know how positive rumour tends to be. Rumour will have a buy-out by a group of ex-horse-butchers from the Ukraine, intent on firing two-thirds of the workforce on the spot and putting the rest on half-rations, pay-wise. Lack of consultation means staff being sent on computer skills courses to learn new systems even though they appear of less use and value than existing ones.

No wonder staff get stressed.

Presenteeism

Long hours are stressful, especially when they produce low output. Which is why the cult of presenteeism is a named suspect in the list of causes of stress. It is a 'bums-on-seats' culture where staff believe they need to be seen to be working early and late. God knows how it started, although the Japanese seem to be best at it.

Bad or Absent Leadership

Good business leaders are as rare as hen's teeth. Some duff ones have their moment of glory but most have no idea what a leader is or what he/she is supposed to do. Many firms sail rudderless because no one seems to have the term 'leader' in their job description.

Staff need a good leader to survive as a functioning, successful team. I have seen workers on paltry pay with unrewarding jobs who are still able to sustain a happy and fulfilling work environment because of good leadership. An effective, charismatic leader can take people through hell or high water simply because their passion is contagious. People who work for good leaders are confident in their roles. They have trust and they are aware of objectives. They get recognition and reward. They are therefore less likely to suffer from workplace-related stress.

Good leaders are visible, not virtual. Good leaders don't lead from boardrooms or meeting rooms. Good leaders don't lead working from home. They don't lead if they sit at their computers all day, tapping in figures. They also don't lead if they are constantly globetrotting.

Work–Life Balance

You're expecting this to be the stress-busting bit. Work–life balance has been hailed as the saviour to work stress. Get out of the office and go play with your kids. Get a life. The idea is sound, the practice less so. If you've given body and soul to a career, a life outside the workplace might not be quite so easy just to pick up when you feel like it. A lot depends on how long the neglect has been going on for. Your marriage may have already broken down. Or perhaps you never got married because you were just too busy. Many women put off having children until it fits in with their career, but some are finding that time flew when they were having fun and now it's too late. The biological clock hasn't just ticked by, its batteries have expired.

Many firms embraced the culture of work–life balance without ever giving their staff the tools to achieve it. Like stress management, it was a concept, rather than a working reality. Which means people not only carried on working hard, they started to do so while feeling guilty about not achieving that crucial balance. Guilt turns to stress. The pressure just increased.

Home Stress

So staff use work as an escape from stress at home. Don't think everyone loitering in the office after six o'clock is necessarily a corporate victim. Count the number of toddlers in the photos on their desks. Now imagine the auditory output from those grinning, gummy little mouths. The office may be a haven by comparison.

Tips for Avoiding Workplace Stress

Be realistic

♦ Only work late when you have to.

♦ Take regular breaks, even if they only last a few minutes.

◆ Take time for mental reflection. Allow a period of quiet to warm up prior to starting work in the morning, and a period of quiet to take stock in the evening.

◆ If you can't change it, let it drop.

◆ Stop allowing people to annoy, irritate, depress, frustrate or humiliate you. *You're* in charge of your moods and emotions, not them.

◆ When you start to worry about work, remember how much time in your life you have spent worrying about things that never happened.

◆ If you think a work problem feels like a matter of life or death, imagine how it would feel if you'd just won six million on the lottery.

◆ Repeat after me: 'Life's too short'.

◆ And: 'I feel calm, confident and in control'.

◆ Learn the skill of taking a moment. Pause. Breathe out. *Don't* take it personally.

Change the scene

◆ If you can, go and look out of the window for a reflective break. Look at the sky. Look at the clouds. Watch trees or other people in other offices, or rabbits playing on the verge. Anything that isn't the environment you are working in.

◆ Go for a ride in the lift. Get out and look at the view, if possible. (Don't jump.)

◆ Go and sit in the loo.

◆ Go out and buy an ice lolly or a bag of popcorn. Eat it sitting on a bench, if you can.

Coping with problems

◆ Life is all about problems. It's up to you to decide how to deal with them. You can either set about solving them or sit around moaning about them.

◆ Stop moaning.

◆ Learn to accept what you can't change. If you can't solve the problems, let them drop.

◆ Write your feelings down in your Little Book of Madness. Take time to write some nice feelings down too.

◆ Talk the boss into letting you have a game of table football in the restroom. Ten minutes spent playing against a colleague will ensure you are laughing again.

◆ Allow yourself to make mistakes. Nobody's perfect. The bigger the brain, the sillier the mistake.

◆ If your job is dealing with complaints, learn the core skills of people management. Be clever at those skills but remember: some people are impossible. Don't take it personally. Be polite, helpful and professional. Nobody can do more than that.

Leaving it all behind

◆ Avoid taking work problems home with you. They pollute what should be your refuge. Imagine you are entering a decontamination unit on the way through the door. At home you laugh, talk and bicker as a family. What you don't do is bore and depress others with the comparative trivia of your day.

◆ Work it off with exercise, instead. Walk quickly on the way home, jog round the block, walk the dog, swim, dance, skip with a rope, have sex – anything other than sitting there moaning.

- When you walk in the door, change the script. Think of something else to talk about – anything funny or interesting. Rack your brains. Make it your challenge. It will feel phoney and it will feel alien, but it will start to change your mood.

- On the way home, instead of rushing to work-whinge with your partner, start to focus on – and look forward to – the good things that you are going to do when you get there. Anticipation is over 50 per cent of the enjoyment of anything. Think of that nice cup of Earl Grey, or that chilled glass of wine. Plan for that episode of *ER* or think about laughing as you bath the kids. Take something home to ensure you are perceived as a fun person, rather than the usual ratbag. Buy a funny hat or a set of comics, including one for your partner. Play a joke. Phone on the way home and make them laugh. Announce your good mood just as strongly as you would normally announce your bad one.

- If you live alone, think of someone you can phone, with the objective of making them laugh. Keep the call short in case they work a long day too.

- Don't go home and start surfing the Internet. It's too much like what you've been doing all day.

- Treat yourself to a few 'at home' outfits. Make sure you look nice during your leisure time. By wearing scruffy clothes that make you look bad you are making the leisure time feel and look unimportant. Dressing up for it, even in casual soft-wear, will make it register in your mind as an occasion in the day, rather than time to be passed between going to work. Watch programmes like *Friends*. Americans are much better at 'At-home' wear than we are. They buy things like cute pyjama-style bottoms and matching sweatshirt tops and soft-wear shorts that manage to look attractive but comfy at the same time. You'd actually look forward to getting home to change into them and your partner would still find you attractive. The same can't be said for baggy joggers and ancient, stonewashed jeans.

Keeping on top of it all

♦ Avoid stress-inducing foods. Caffeine is a stimulant and will stay in the bloodstream for hours. It is present in coffee, tea, chocolate and cola drinks. Treat yourself to one or two cups of really good coffee per day and then stick to water, fruit juices, herb tea or decaff.

♦ Learn to be assertive. Self-resentment brews when you allow yourself to be a doormat.

♦ Delegate.

♦ Spend 15 minutes per week drawing pictures of the things that are stressing you out. Then tear the drawings up.

♦ Start telling people about the things you like and enjoy, not just the things that piss you off.

♦ Give your PC a cute name. It will make you less hostile when it doesn't do what you want. People rarely rant at or hit their mouse because it reminds them of a furry little creature.

♦ Be less judgemental of others – build low expectations. People are human with all the accompanying moods, eccentricities and foibles. If you expect them to be perfect you will become less tolerant.

Praising and caring for yourself

♦ Try to lighten the mood among your team when possible. Fun-free zones breed stress.

♦ Praise as well as criticise. It will make you feel better and may produce the same response in others.

♦ Praise yourself and reward work done well.

♦ Group together all the jobs and phone calls that are stressing you out and blitz them when you are in a high-energy mood.

◆ Ask for help when you need it.

◆ Take time off sick when you are ill.

◆ Suggest your firm allows two 'duvet days' per year, i.e. days allowed off when you aren't ill but just need a break.

◆ Make friendships in the workplace but maintain or grow friendships outside, too. Ditto romantic and/or sexual relationships. Otherwise the phrase 'all your eggs in one basket' springs to mind. Convenient though it might be, it is healthier to spread your options a little. Financial job-dependency is one thing, but emotional and relationship job-dependency is a lot more sinister. To manage your stress levels you should be trying to see work as something other than your entire universe. This is hard if that is exactly what it has become.

Relax

◆ Avoid hacking away on your laptop as you commute.

◆ Read and watch comedy, light entertainment, or escapist stuff. Keep away from work-related topics. If you move from the financial and business sections to the TV news to *Newsnight* via *The Manager's Guide to Finance* then you deserve the breakdown that is heading your way.

◆ Have hobbies that are in direct opposition to your job: if you have a non-productive occupation, like marketing, admin or accountancy then you need a hobby where you will produce an end product, like baking, DIY, pottery or gardening.

◆ If your job is non-creative try painting, drawing, writing poems, collage or interior design.

◆ If you have a quiet job then singing or learning to play the drums will be therapeutic.

◆ If you spend all week masking your emotions have a go at paint-balling or funfair rides that make you yell.

♦ If you have creative-thinking employment then go for something more logical, like puzzles, researching the family tree or car maintenance.

♦ The more adult you have to be in your job, the more childish your activities should be.

Healing at Source

You can also try any, or all, of the whole raft of stress-busting treatments, from aromatherapy to massage to playing with your corporate stress ball. These are a nice way to pass the time and most of them are very relaxing. To learn to control your stress response, though, you need to heal from source.

Stress is the body's response to life-or-death situations. It is fight or flight. It is primarily for survival. It is actually a good thing for your body to do under the appropriate circumstances. If you were being attacked by a wild beast then the accelerated heartbeat, short, rapid breathing, muscle tension, shutdown of all body functions apart from the most vital for action and that rush of adrenaline would make you faster and stronger.

The problem with workplace stress, though, is that it's not a wild beast, it's just another complaining client. Or a business presentation you've got to make. Or the photocopier needs filling and no one else has bothered. When the stimulus is inappropriate, then so is the response. Accelerated heartbeat becomes palpitations, increased breathing turns into hyperventilation. Muscle tension becomes headaches, shoulder aches and backache. Your digestive system shuts down. Your bladder wants to empty. Things start to spin out of control and your emotional response is magnified.

We need to start with the mental process. If the stimulus can be put into context then the response will lessen or even disappear. If you can convince yourself this situation isn't a matter of life and death, that you're not being chased by a wild beast, that it is only a delayed train or a demanding boss, then the symptoms will lessen.

Work on Your Perception First

Emergencies in the workplace need to be stimulating, but they shouldn't start to destroy us. We should put a limit on our panic. There needs to be a bottom line of calm. It's good to get a flicker of excitement or even concern when you think about a challenging task. It's not good when that flicker becomes an inferno and makes you unable to cope.

Which is why I go back to my original point: have fun. Remember to laugh. Take breaks. Take stock. Study the true meaning of life. What are the only things worth getting anxious about? The answer is usually health and relationships. Work is important, more so to some than others. If you are stressed you will be unable to do that work effectively. Duck and dive.

Weeding Out the Worthies

We all know many of the things that stress us out at work are simply not worth it. You need to learn to disempower them. What you will start doing from now on is making decisions. As each problem, irritant or pressure-stimulant rears its ugly head you are going to make a quick call over whether it is worth your health and mental well-being or not. This speedy selection process is going to be called the 'stuff-it' decision.

Between the stimulus and your own response there is a gap. The two are not irretrievably interlinked. You have a choice. You can take control. It's up to you whether your response will be negative or positive. When you study your options you will add in a new one: stuff it. This option subdivides into two simple procedures:

1 Do it and stuff it

This will be your self-command for jobs you decide to tackle and for problems you confront and work to overcome, but without the emotional input of stress, worry and anxiety. You are telling yourself to do the job, but not to allow it to be emotionally affecting.

2 Stuff it

This will be your self-command for things you decide are better untackled, like that unflattering comment about yourself that you overheard, or that colleague who pinched your idea and took the glory. These are the stimulants that are going to provoke no tangible or emotional response at all. You are just going to let them drop. When you let them drop you will also let drop your own resentment, anger, irritation, angst, etc. You have decided it is just not worth it.

And no – I know it's not easy to merely dismiss stress like that. But it *is* the best mental exercise if you want to offload. Marry it with practical steps, like better time management and assertiveness and you will be well on the way to keeping your stress at comfortable levels.

Coping With Others' Stress

Of course, it could be that your stress levels are already negligible. Perhaps your problem with workplace stress stems from your colleagues' behaviour, rather than your own. When I talk at seminars I often discover many members of the audience have come to find out about dealing with the stress that is around them, rather than their own.

Stress can be contagious. It is hard to work in an environment of headless chickens without becoming one yourself. If members of your team constantly work as though someone's set off the fire alarm, then it's probably true that the quality of your output will be suffering as a result. You can't inflict calm. You can't order it and you can't spread it as quickly as stress. Telling people to 'calm down' makes them worse. Asking someone if they are stressed will often make them go into denial. If you sit as an oasis of chilled-out calm yourself you will probably drive your colleagues further up the stress pole.

If you are a manager you need to monitor the stress levels of the rest of your team. Not only will they be functioning less effectively, they may also become unwell. Stress is an expensive problem for business, both in terms of days off sick and some-times litigation. Time management will become zero if the team is very stressed. Decisions take longer or bad ones are made too quickly. Medium-size problems appear insurmountable. Team dynamics erode rapidly. Spats break out. People are uncoopera-tive. Take avoiding action:

◆ Look at hours worked without breaks.

◆ Look at communications – is your team briefed? Does it understand the goals?

◆ Do you praise and motivate team members? Is their hard work being acknowledged?

◆ Are you an inspirational leader?

◆ Are you fair? Do you have favourites? Are some of the team rewarded more than others? Are any being allowed to be carried as dead weight?

◆ Are they able to communicate with you? If they are stressed can they come and tell you?

◆ Have you tried doing a stress audit?

◆ Do you have procedures in place if a member of staff reports suffering from stress, or would you just tell them to take a couple of days off?

- Do you encourage your team to have fun from time to time? Do you ease the pressure?

- Do you work to each individual's main motivational factor? Are you aware what it is they enjoy most in their job and where they achieve the maximum reward?

- Does your team trust you?

Organising Crises – Hot, Stress-busting Tips

- Make a time log of workplace emergencies. Work out how much of your day they occupy.

- Be more pro-active. Most crises could have been spotted and diverted. Build a risk-assessment facility into your thinking. Don't hope something won't happen, build in a contingency plan in case it does.

- Don't overreact. Not all problems are crises.

- Crisis-plan into your journey times. Don't be surprised that trains get cancelled or traffic builds up.

- Watch out for queues. We spend, on average, 73 hours per year in queues. Plan to avoid them (shop early or late) and, when you do hit them, keep calm. Use the time to meditate on bigger issues.

- If your team work best when something goes wrong then they are working badly. Instead of managing the crisis, they should be tracking back, discovering how it happened, and making sure it doesn't happen again.

- Get rid of all the clocks in the workplace. Evidently without clocks around we are less stressed and work more naturally.

- Start to assess your work in terms of results, rather than effort or time. Encourage your bosses and colleagues to do the same.

- ◆ Stop writing things down on old envelopes. Get a proper notebook.

- ◆ Stress makes you chaotic. Spurn starchy, sugary foods for protein-rich meals, plus a vitamin B complex supplement as this nutrient depletes when we are stressed.

- ◆ Look busy during a 'wander break'.

- ◆ When you are working at your desk, stop for a regular 'tidy-break'. This gives you an opportunity to refocus your thinking, rest your body and get rid of the clutter, all at the same time.

CHAPTER SIX

Assertiveness

Quick Tips

- ◆ Work out what is and what isn't negotiable.

- ◆ Avoid backing below your bottom line (pressurised into doing something that you've said you can't do).

- ◆ Never use 'No' or 'Can't' unless you mean them.

- ◆ Be clear and concise.

- ◆ Deal with the other person's feelings or needs first to create rapport.

- ◆ Tell them what you want.

- ◆ Be polite but firm.

- ◆ Be honest about what's relevant.

- ◆ Avoid emotional displays.

- ◆ Be flexible – negotiate.

- ◆ Work adult to adult.

- ◆ Take a problem-solving stance.

- ◆ Tackle time-consuming problems at source. Don't put them off.

- ◆ Never accept more work than you can finish – renegotiation should not be an option.

- ◆ Be calm.

The art of being firm is very time-productive. Why? Well, being assertive helps clean up time-leaks in the following four key areas:

1. You learn how to say no. This means you get control over your own diary and workload.

2. You cut to the quick verbally. You learn to be more honest and productive in your communications. Much business time wastage is caused by unclear, misunderstood communications.

3. You learn to drop your own emotional baggage and how to treat others in a way that is less likely to cause friction.

4. You become less stressed. Aggressive and passive behaviours both cause stress. Aggressive people stress out their colleagues and passive people stress themselves out.

Childish Responses

We learn behavioural responses as a child. Put simply, we work on a reward and return basis. If a tactic works we tend to stick at it, unless shown otherwise. Children tend to carry an armoury of only two responses to a situation they don't like: fight or flight, i.e. aggression or passivity. Fail to give a child the chocolate it wants and it may throw a temper tantrum. If this results in it being given the chocolate it will have learned a valuable lesson about future tactics.

I was brought up to believe that good little girls do as they are told. They are quiet and well behaved. I received praise, reward and affection for behaving in this manner. I couldn't understand my aggressive little cousin. His behaviour was naughty and he got a smack. Why would he carry on doing that? I felt silence was a winning formula. Adulthood should lead us to a more results-orientated behavioural option: being assertive. This is objective-led thinking and behaviour. It looks long term. It is part of a 'respond, not react' philosophy. Look at the bigger picture, rather than settling for short-term gain.

Yet we still insist on using the passive–aggressive options. Why? Because they work. Aggressive people usually get results. Passive people avoid conflict by doing what they are told. So why change? Here are the reasons:

Aggressive Behaviour

♦ Creates resentment.

♦ Makes you unpopular.

♦ Creates unwillingness in others.

♦ Causes conflict.

♦ Destroys loyalty.

♦ Causes stress in both you and your colleagues.

♦ Gets you sued if it is classed as bullying or harassment.

♦ Makes you a bad time-manager.

Effects of aggressive behaviour on your time management

♦ You have to keep checking jobs and people because they will only do what they are told and no more.

♦ You have to work with people who dislike you and may be disruptive to your schedules.

♦ You have to dominate at all times.

♦ You upset people, which makes them slower.

♦ You tend to talk too 'straight', getting people's backs up by speaking your mind without using tact.

♦ You have to go back and apologise for your own thoughtlessness.

◆ You feel guilty, which prevents focused thought.

◆ You go into denial and blame others for your own negative outcomes, destabilising relationships and hindering teamwork.

Passive Behaviour

◆ Destroys confidence.

◆ Destroys inner self-esteem.

◆ Lets you get treated as a doormat.

◆ Makes you take on unachievable deadlines and workloads.

◆ Makes others uncomfortable.

◆ Causes inner resentment.

◆ Causes stress.

◆ Makes you a bad time-manager.

Effects of passive behaviour on your time management

◆ You waste time doing jobs you have accepted and which you know you should have turned down.

◆ You have no way of prioritising and getting your decisions accepted.

◆ You are out of control of everything, including your diary.

◆ Your inner resentment affects your clarity of thought and purpose.

◆ Your communications are indirect. People rarely know what you mean.

◆ People get irritated by you and distrust you because you aren't 'talking straight'.

Passive–Aggressive

This is a frequent optional response. You allow yourself to be used as a doormat. You say 'yes' to everything that lands on your desk. You seethe inside because you are being 'used' by others. Then – after a long period of passivity – you blow your stack. You say your piece and let them have it with both barrels. All those years of resentment, and now it's pay-back time. This behaviour is alarming and unfair. The response is out of proportion to the offence. You have dragged in all your old emotional baggage, all the stuff that has been festering inside for years. Let's face it, we've all been there.

Assertiveness

This is known as 'levelling' behaviour because it keeps the relationship or transaction on an even keel, adult to adult. It means you stand up for your own rights but allow others theirs as well. By expressing yourself concisely and directly you save time because you get your point across. People understand you and you listen to and understand them. Being assertive means avoiding misunderstandings, and misunderstanding is one of the biggest business Time Bandits around.

It helps you move problems forward positively, rather than dwelling on them and spending time in 'what if?' mode. Nobody wins, nobody loses. Everybody is happy. Sound difficult? Well, it is. Remember that 'assertive' doesn't describe a person, it describes their behaviour. It is an option, not a constant. Your behaviour will probably be a mix of appropriate – or inappropriate – options. You chose when to be assertive. You can also choose not to be.

To be assertive you will be:

- Flexible
- Fair
- Honest about what's relevant
- Calm

- Logical
- Able to see the other person's viewpoint
- Objective-led
- Moving towards a solution
- Listening
- Creating empathy

To be aggressive you will be:

- Loud
- Patronising
- Failing to allow others to hold opinions or disagree with your viewpoint
- Attacking
- Critical
- Invading space and territory
- Ganging up
- Using insults
- Dominating conversations

To be passive you will be:

- Quiet
- Sitting at the back in groups
- Agreeing with others for a quiet life
- Apologetic
- Talking yourself down
- Doing things you don't want to do
- Acting as a doormat

Non-assertive dialogues include phrases like:

- 'Sorry.'
- 'This may sound stupid, but . . .'
- 'I know it probably isn't my place, but . . .'
- 'If you like . . .'

- 'I don't mind.'
- 'That's typical of me, always getting it wrong . . .'
- 'I know you won't like this . . .'
- 'He made me feel nervous.'
- 'I could never complain.'
- 'I'm *just* a PA.'
- 'I *only* manage a small team.'

Flawed Responses

When we get into a transaction with anyone we listen to our inner voice. This voice will monitor our progress and tell us how we are doing. The problem with that voice is it is biased. It is only on one side. It is also affected by past transactions and keen to spot repeat patterns. It tries to make order out of chaos. It looks for sets of triggers to stimulate a pre-programmed set of responses. Even if those responses haven't worked in the past it will still insist on using them because that is the pattern that has been incurred.

Some flawed responses that occur on a serial basis include:

1 Over-dramatising

As in:

- 'That's *terrible!*'
- 'She's a complete bitch.'
- 'He's an awful person.'
- 'I know my boss hates me.'
- 'I was absolutely *devastated.*'

2 Negativity

As in:

- 'I know he said my work was good but what he *really* meant was it was terrible before.'

- 'She said she liked my hair but I could tell she was lying.'
- 'The figures are up this week but let's see them drop like a stone next week.'

3 Catastrophising

As in:

- 'If I can't get those figures by five I'm dead.'
- 'He'll never talk to me again if I don't get this done on time.'
- 'We're sunk if we don't move on this one.'

4 Seeing patterns

As in:

- 'I *always* get in the longest queue.'
- 'I *never* get taken seriously at meetings.'
- 'He only ever criticises me.'
- 'It *always* rains when I forget my umbrella.'

Patterns of Conflict

Take your average domestic row. Often this will be over something relatively trivial. Sometimes it will be over a serial misdemeanour. The same problem again, so your brain spots the pattern and comes up with the set response. It knows the response was ineffective every other time but it is not going to be called a quitter. You say the same thing. You have the same row. This pattern can repeat and repeat throughout your marriage or relationship. Parents do it with children. Bosses do it with employees.

Being assertive means breaking these patterns if they're not working. The rules of engagement with assertiveness are:

1. Know your overall objective.

2. Know your subobjectives, if you have any.

3. Know what is and isn't negotiable – stick to your bottom line.

4. Analyse your own feelings and see if they will help or hinder the transaction. If they will hinder (and they probably will, in my experience) move them off the field of play for the time being.

5. Work out how the other person must be feeling.

6. Be calm.

7. Be flexible.

8. Create empathy.

9. Take care of the other person first.

10. Tell them what you want and/or how you feel.

11. Negotiate a solution.

Time-management Situations in Business Where Assertiveness Can Help

1 Negotiating your workload

A manager arrives with a job that she says is 'urgent'. You already have a full schedule. She tells you she wants priority.

Passive response: take it and agree to do it first. Allow the other jobs to be put on the back burner.

Aggressive response: tell her you're too busy. Why can't she give it to one of the others for a change? Or *sarcasm*: 'I suppose you think I'm just sitting around here with nothing to do?'

Passive–aggressive response: accept it but do it in your own time.

Assertive response: create empathy first. Acknowledge how urgent the job is. Show concern and understanding, without sounding patronising. Then tell her you are sorry but you have other jobs waiting. Then negotiate. Tell her when you could do it.

2 Taking on extra work

One of your team has left/been made redundant. You have been told you will have to take over her workload.

Passive response: accept the situation and work late to get the job done.

Aggressive response: tell them you won't help. If your boss wanted a doormat he should have bought one from Woolworths.

Passive–aggressive response: agree, but moan bitterly and constantly. Say you expect more money or you'll leave too.

Assertive response: again, show empathy. Tell them you understand there is extra work to share out and that you are willing to help. Explain how much you are prepared to take on, and ask how that will reflect in your salary. Negotiate.

3 Dealing with time-wasters

A colleague comes to sit on your desk each morning and spends an average of 20 minutes moaning about his manager. You sympathise, but you have work to do.

Passive response: sit and listen, panicking inside.

Aggressive response: tell him you're too busy. Did he know he wastes 1.5 hours per week whingeing? You've got work to be getting on with, even if he hasn't.

Passive–aggressive response: pretend to be busy and ignore him. Move offices. Get someone to call you away urgently each time. Tell him your boss has banned you from chatting.

Assertive response: tell him he has your full sympathy and you can understand the need to offload. However, you can never give him your full attention because your own workload is so heavy. You simply don't have the time to spare. What if you stopped off for coffee once a week to give him your undivided attention?

Some quickies

1. Your boss is a poor communicator and gives you tasks with little in the way of explanation. As a consequence you often find yourself muddling through using guesswork or spending time correcting your own mistakes.

   Assertive response: make an appointment to sit down with your boss. Avoid accusatory phrases like: 'You always ...' or 'You probably don't realise ...' or 'You must ...'. Tell him/her that you know they are busy but that it would be a tremendous help to you if he/she could go into a little more detail when explaining tasks. Try not to harp on about past problems, but focus on future behaviours. Be as specific as possible. Say how long you need with him/her, or tell your boss the type of extra information that would be useful. Give them a WIIFM? (what's in it for me?) factor by pointing out the benefits to your boss of this change in behaviour. Tell him/her it will enable you to speed the job up or be more accurate.

2. You job-share with a colleague. She isn't pulling her weight and you feel your time is being used correcting her mistakes or dealing with problems she should have got through.

   Assertive response: arrange a meeting with this woman and try to do so in the flesh. Tell her you know she must get busy during her shift, but ask if she realised you were inheriting a lot of her problems. Ask if the same ever happens to her and whether you can both work out a compromise so that the job runs more smoothly for both of you.

3. Your boss always waits until 5.00 pm to start rushing up with 'urgent' jobs. This means you have to work late on a regular basis.

Assertive response: don't tackle the past by using words like 'always' and 'you never'. Aim for future improvement. Tell her you'd be able to do a better job on them if you weren't rushing. Could you go to her at 4.00 pm to check for late jobs? Could she prioritise the ones that could be left for the morning? Offer to help towards a compromise. Avoid making accusations.

4. Your IT department is slow at responding to calls for help. When someone does turn up he/she rushes through the problem, leaving you in the dark about what to do next time.

Assertive response: find a time when they aren't busy and pop down for a chat. Try to build a relationship that isn't always based on crisis. Get to know them as part of the team. Tell them you would perhaps have to call them out less if they could take a few moments to explain how you could solve the problem yourself next time. Show you are keen for knowledge. Write down any instructions. Ask them what sort of way they like problems described over the phone. Learn the jargon they like to work in.

5. You are handling customer complaints over the phone. You try to give undivided attention but certain clients take a long time repeating their points. You have a set amount of customers to deal with in an hour and the others are queuing up.

Assertive response: two options here: either speak to your supervisor and tell him/her your call-handling targets are not achievable unless you cut customers off mid-call. Say you feel this makes them more agitated and that a little longer to listen and speak would make them more satisfied, which will cut down on complaints. Or: be more assertive with the customer. Interrupt if you are forced to, using their name as an attention grabber. Be polite and apologise for having to stop them. Build in a benefit to them. Tell them you need to get some quick details to deal with their problem more speedily. Empathise with their emotions first.

You are within your rights to tell people how you feel about a situation. The point is you should do so in a way that is calm. You can describe the emotion without acting it out, e.g.: 'I feel very angry when you speak to me like that' or: 'It upsets me to hear you think I am not pulling my weight on this job.'

6. You need to close down a long winded-meeting.

Assertive response: be firm, especially if the meeting is lively. Stand, if the others are sitting. Talk over them if you need to create a gap. This is not a time for etiquette by the book. Or raise your hands, palms to front. Say there is obviously more to be discussed but that time is running out. Would they like you to reschedule with this subject top of the agenda? Be apologetic but firm. Don't make anyone feel they have been made to look long-winded or childish.

Offering Criticism

◆ Be specific in outlining the behaviour you want changed. Avoid vague phrases, like: 'You're not pulling your weight' or 'You're too lazy'. The first doesn't detail what you mean and the second is a statement of fact, rather than a comment intended to produce improvement.

◆ Point out some positives as well as negatives.

- Give facts, not opinions.

- Listen to their point of view.

- Never make personal comments.

- Be tactful, but come to the point.

- Be calm.

- Be personal in your opinions. Say '*I* think', rather than 'They think' or 'We think'.

- Never use sarcasm.

- State what you expect as an outcome of the discussion.

- Don't use criticism to wound or gain points. Only use it to seek improvement.

Taking Criticism

- Listen.

- Ask for details.

- Ask for facts.

- Reflect key points back to clarify.

- Don't argue.

- Don't become defensive.

- Don't reply with attack.

- Stay calm.

Body Language

Being assertive isn't just a verbal dialogue, though. It needs to be reflected in your tone and your body language to appear suitable, i.e. for you to look as though you mean it.

Passive bodytalk

- No eye contact
- Head down
- Folded arms or other barriers
- Fiddling
- Hesitant or rushed speech
- Over-smiling
- Drooped shoulders

Aggressive bodytalk

- Staring
- Frowning
- Pointing
- Looming over others
- Looking bored while they talk
- Hands behind head, feet on desk
- Tapping
- Hands into fists
- Hands on hips
- High arm-fold
- Head tilted back

Assertive bodytalk

- Upright posture
- Eye contact
- Appropriate smile
- Listening gestures
- Open gestures

Coping With Behavioural Change

Humans are complex and so are their responses. Assertive behaviour is all about adult-to-adult transactions; behaving with dignity and treating your colleagues with respect. But a perfect world it isn't. Old patterns from childhood can kick in just when you don't expect them. A conversation may be going well and moving to a positive conclusion, saving all concerned acres of time. Then one thing is said and responded to. Emotional baggage is triggered and suddenly you're on the brink of World War III.

A recurring theme of this book is: respond don't react. You need to plan your transactions like a chess game and know where to move to when the response is negative. Nobody is the world expert on this one, except on paper. I have met some of the gurus of behavioural analysis, and – believe me – they can create just as much transactional dross as the next person. One person I know spends much of her time researching and teaching the subject and the rest rubbing her colleagues up the wrong way.

Emotions are a powerful force to wrestle with, especially when they are your own. Remember the message, though: when emotions threaten to hinder a transaction you must move them off the field of play.

Stimulus–react is a form of useless verbal ping-pong. They say one thing and your response is driven by emotions, not logic. You indulge in banter. You both make wounding or non-helpful remarks. You enter patterns from child–adult relationships. Whose turn it is to be the adult and whose to be the child is largely up to you.

Learned Responses

There are six main categories of behaviour or response. Three are adult and three childish. Three can be useful in business and three are a constant hindrance. The six categories are:

Positive

1. *Adult:* the assertive option – logical, problem-solving, unemotional, encouraging, fair-minded, flexible, calm.

2. *Nurturing Parent:* helpful, mentoring, caring, training, giving advice, encouraging, sets limits, firm, soothing, supportive.

3. *Free Child:* spirited, keen, honest, sharing emotions, tells you their feelings, enthusiastic, tells you their wants and needs.

Negative

4. *Critical Parent:* opinionated, believes he/she is right and know better, criticises mistakes, unwilling to delegate because little faith in others, sarcastic, tells people what's wrong with them, gives opinions, rather than facts.

5. *Rebellious Child:* aggressive, dominant, stubborn, refuses to co-operate, rebels even when this is at odds with what he wants.

6. *Compliant Child:* passive, avoids or runs away, does what others want, keen to please even when displeases self.

Very few people lead their entire lives in any one state. Like the passive/aggressive/assertive options, they describe behaviour, rather than people. I can easily move through all of them during the duration of one blisteringly good row. My all-time favourite at home is Rebellious Child. I could win medals for sulking and stubbornness. Sulking and stubbornness are both classic Time Bandits, though. At work you need to unlock sooner. You should crawl out of Rebellious Child and into Adult asap.

The trick in business is to avoid the negative options for a fruitful transaction. Remember behaviour breeds behaviour. Look at the way your transaction is going. Imagine the Critical Parent state and relate it to your own experiences of behavioural 'patterns', especially from childhood. Were you ever told: 'You've *got* to clean up your room, it looks like a pigsty'? What state did that dialogue move you into? Adult? Hell no! Orders like that, backed up with an insult, would have sent you scampering into Rebellious Child as fast as your little legs could take you. Then the parent would make that vital mistake: 'You've got to do it, or else.'

That one sentence guaranteed a visit from the environmental health officer at a later stage. It invited stubbornness.

Yet we still produce similar patterns later in life. Parents should be brilliant at parent–child transactions but they rarely are because most of them only learn what *doesn't* work, not what does.

Study the transactional states and hear the warning bells when you either experience or start using any of the negative ones. Then plan your move. If Critical Parent has just dug you into a hole, climb out of it by moving into Adult, Nurturing Parent, or Free Child. If you find you've just been on the receiving end of Critical Parent, stop yourself before you move into Rebellious Child. Study the options and think of the expected response.

No behaviour comes with a lifetime's guarantee to be effective but negative behaviour comes with a guarantee to cause disruption and therefore eats into your valuable time.

PART TWO

Practical Skills

CHAPTER SEVEN

Prioritising and Delegating

Prioritising creates structure and time-efficiency. Delegation then becomes a vital tool to ensure you don't get bogged down in a welter of 'can do' and overwork.

Quick Tips

- ◆ Know your core objective: what is it I am paid to do?

- ◆ Ask: what is the best use of my time right now?

- ◆ Sell your objectives to yourself first. If you are unconvinced, so will others be.

- ◆ Study and list both long- and short-term goals.

- ◆ Clarify the difference between 'Urgent' and 'Important'. Donate time to the 'Important' task. If a job's just 'Urgent' do it straight away but don't dedicate much time to it.

- ◆ Once you have learnt which jobs you can pass on, learn to delegate.

Prioritising

This relatively simple skill underpins your entire time-management programme. If your day is demand driven it runs to chaos. Demands are rarely the same thing as priorities.

Pare back to the bone. In the first part of the book you did some soul-searching about your life and what is important in it. Now we are going to create the ultimate order. Write down, in no more than one sentence, what it is you are in your job to do. What are you paid for? What is your core objective?

Now, once you have that clear, concise and written in front of you I want you to make it official. Get the sentence printed. Laminate it, if necessary. And pin it somewhere where you can see it. You get busy and you need a reminder: 'These are my prime objectives.' Prioritise your workload accordingly. Use these core values to remind others in your team, too.

Another phrase to use on yourself regularly: 'What is the best use of my time right now?'

You will need to communicate and sell these priorities to your colleagues. But the first person you will need to sell them to is yourself. If they don't work for you, you will soon start to work off-piste. I meet many managers, in particular, who refuse to delegate tasks because they see their priority job to be one of *doing*, not *managing*. They fail to understand the role of a manager. They feel guilty keeping management as a time priority, possibly because they don't understand what the job entails. Managing is something they hope to do if and when they have a gap in the day. Yet managing should be a priority in itself. Imagine if the pilot of a plane failed to prioritise. What if he/she noticed they were a steward short and the customers weren't getting their drinks? What if he/she started helping out with the trolley, instead of flying the plane?

Prioritise to prevent:

◆ Constantly having to dig yourself out of holes.

◆ Caving in to external pressure from others in your life.

◆ Accepting unrealistic deadlines.

◆ Buckling under the pressure of eternal crises.

Goal Arranging

Structure your goals and priorities under two columns: long and short term.

Long-term goals

Start to plan each of these with a series of questions:

1. How hard will this be to achieve?

2. What will I need to achieve it?

3. What planning will I need to do?

4. What actions will I need to take? (Subdivide these into *Global*, i.e. planned, big-step actions, like taking training or doing research, and *Linear* steps, i.e. smaller stages, like sending away for the training prospectus or logging on to the Internet.)

5. What do I need to be taught?

6. What help will I need to enlist?

7. What mindset will I need? What emotions will I need to use/avoid?

8. What is my motivation?

9. What will remotivate me through short-term failures or barriers?

10. What do I need to plan as a back pocket in case of emergencies?

Short-term goals

This will be your to-do list. Subdivide into three headings:

1. Goals

2. Tasks

3. Actions

Four-box Planning

Once you begin to do the big-picture prioritising you can start to set about the smaller stuff, too. Any jobs that fall on to your desk need to be judged in terms of your overall objectives. Bring them back to your personal mission statement, that sheet of paper that tells you what you are there for. Look at that sentence and grade them accordingly. The quickest and best way to deal with jobs and paperwork is to grade them under four headings:

1 Urgent and important

These are tasks and paperwork that fit into your 'high priority' profile, and which need to be dealt with urgently.

2 Important, not urgent

These jobs fulfil your 'high priority' profile, but don't need to be dealt with straight away. Make sure you file or load them correctly, though. They need to be in a 'bring forward' file or they could get neglected and become a time emergency. Work out how you can delay these deadlines or file them.

3 Urgent, not important

These jobs lie outside your priority criteria. They often shout the loudest, though. Delegation is the key skill needed here. If you don't have planned time to deal with them find someone else who has. If you have to handle them yourself make sure you do them quickly. Allot the minimum time for each 'urgent, not important task'. They should not merit large-scale time gaps, which should be reserved for your 'urgent and important' tasks only. Negotiate this part of your workload. Work on your assertiveness skills.

4 Not important, not urgent

These are low-level priority tasks and you should avoid wasting time on them.

Hot Tips for Prioritising

◆ Keep your core objective pinned on the wall beside you. If you're not sure how to prioritise ask how the job aligns to this objective.

◆ If you have an unclear authority situation in your office, keep a chart of who has authority for what.

◆ Clarify your departmental objectives with your boss.

◆ If you have multiple bosses, ask each for clarification of priority tasks. Work like a hospital waiting room. Keep visual reminders of your current workload on your desk, e.g. a written chart showing your current priority task and how many are on the waiting list. This will allow people delegating you work to see how long the wait will be and may make them decide to delegate elsewhere. It will endorse your words when you tell them you are already busy.

◆ Grow a beard or stop shaving your legs. We spend on average ten weeks of our lives making ourselves clean-shaven.

◆ Stop sleeping. You spend about 20 years of your life asleep.

◆ Stop moaning. Three good whinge-sessions a day and you're notching up nearly 620 days of your life just on getting it all off your chest.

Creating Some Slack

Then, when your priorities are clear in your head, you will need to start creating some slack. You are going to create your first holes. These can be created both at work and at home. To make

holes you are going to pass on some of your workload. To do so effectively you are going to have to learn how to delegate.

Delegating

The ability to delegate is the *bête noire* of frustrated, wannabe time-managers. Too much work on your hands? Why not give it to someone else to do? Simple, isn't it? And yet there are several potential barriers to this simple, unsung skill, including:

1. You are not a manager and therefore have no one to delegate to.

2. Everyone else is too busy with their workload.

3. You try to delegate but no one listens to you.

4. You are too passive to delegate.

5. You try to delegate but find it easier and quicker in the long run to do it yourself.

6. You are too scared to delegate because the buck stops with you and you don't want to absorb the flack for others' mistakes.

7. You do delegate, but then find yourself reclaiming the job later.

8. You're worried you will feel guilty sitting about with others doing all the work.

So, eight little sick notes from your mum, explaining why you can be excused delegation duties. This will mean you are saddled with all the work. Which in turn means you are a poor time-manager.

Delegation for Beginners

Let's suppose you have no formal management role in your job. You have no one beneath you, just bosses and the team that you work with. Can you still delegate?

The answer is – yes, you probably can. Delegation is a skill that does not always require formal authority. You can still manage even if you don't have the word in your job title. Look at the five-way management module that should be relevant to most jobs.

1 Management upwards

If you have a boss you will probably have to manage him or her in some way. At the very least you will be managing the relationship. At the other end of the scale you might be responsible for managing his/her routine and schedule.

Delegating to managers is not as difficult as it sounds. In many ways a quiet but effective revolution is already taking place, thanks to the PC. Many PAs and secretaries have already delegated much of their admin work to their managers. A few years ago few managers would boast 'typing and keyboard skills' on their list of business skills, but these days most of them will now use a keyboard. They create their own filing and do their own correspondence via e-mail. In time many of them will be ready to move on to the next stage of evolutionary development and discover how to make their own coffee.

2 Management outwards

This is the skill of managing clients and suppliers. Delegation has even affected these key relationships. Many companies now use 'partnering' as their way of working with both clients and suppliers. The format is more grown-up, giving both sides more responsibility in the relationship. Companies work hand in hand, rather than along the traditional buyer/supplier lines. Work is delegated accordingly, with a sense of joint responsibility to achieve a common goal.

3 Management sideways

You manage your work and your relationships with your team and your colleagues, and you can delegate to them as well. Your dialogue may be different from the 'ask' or 'order' routine from a boss, and will probably include words like 'would you mind' and 'can you do me a great favour', but the result is often still the same.

4 Management downward

This means working with subordinates, or people who you manage on a more official basis. Delegation to them will be a key requisite of your job.

5 Managing yourself

This is perhaps the hardest area of all. If you can manage yourself you are virtually guaranteed a successful career. This will mean you are calm, logical, forward thinking, fair and reliable. The good thing is you are the only person you will never have to delegate jobs to.

So how do you manage yourself?

Effective delegation requires several key personal skills. You will need to be confident. You will have to be calm. You will want to be a good communicator. It will help if you are a clever negotiator. If you are a red-hot persuader and influencer as well, then consider yourself up and running and set to go. If you lack some of these core skills then your attempts at delegation may be scuppered by your own indecision and the inability of others to either understand or even want to do your tasks.

Delegation via Motivation

There are four ways to get people to do things for you:

1. Ask

2. Tell

3. Threaten

4. Pay

Of the four, tell, threaten and pay sound like the quickest. Give someone an order and – if you have the perceived authority – they will often obey. Bribe them enough and they'll do the same. But they won't be motivated. Motivating people is a long-term time investment.

The boss who bullies will often get things done but that is *all* he or she will get. There is no buy-in. People will do what they are told and no more. If you want to time-manage you will need colleagues to go that extra mile for you now and again.

Delegate, Don't Abdicate

Effective delegation shouldn't mean you pass the task on and then vanish from the scene altogether. If you're worried about inheriting the blame for cock-ups then don't. Keep these two basic points in mind:

1. You can monitor and get feedback. You can still offer help, if needed.

2. You don't just get the blame for cock-ups, you also get to take the praise for work done well.

Who? What? And Why?

Three questions to ask yourself before you get stuck into the motivate–persuade side of delegating:

1. **Who** is the best person to delegate this task to? Does it require core skills? Is it a creative task or a logical one? Who has the time and the talent to tackle it? Is it important or mundane? Is there someone who you want to develop to be better at this type of task?

2. **What** exactly does the job entail? Insufficient or unclear briefing will lead to disaster. Be clear of the overall objectives,

plus the way you want the job done and the timescale in which it needs doing. Set standards and deadlines. Communicate your vision and your criteria for success.

3. **Why** will someone else do this job? Know your own motives. Are you a manager who needs to manage, or someone who has too much to do? Are you delegating to someone who can do the job better? Are you just delegating tasks you don't like? A good delegator will pass on jobs he/she *does* like to do, rather than just clearing their desk of dross. They delegate because it is necessary, not for selfish reasons. Somewhere along the line you will also need to ask WHY the other person will *want* to take your task, too. What's in it for them? What will influence them to accept?

Delegation Checklist

◆ Plan – be clear about the vision, or the task if it is a more everyday task. Know the overall objective.

◆ Decide who will be the best person to do the job.

◆ Be prepared to hand over the entire task.

◆ Make sure you aren't hanging on to any bits of it, just because those are the parts you enjoy.

◆ Think big picture when you estimate time spent on delegation. You may have to invest short-term time on things like training or coaching to save time long term.

◆ Be responsive, not reactive. Don't carry on doing the task yourself just because it's 'easier'.

◆ Learn to trust. Delegating tasks means trusting colleagues.

◆ Communicate effectively. Be honest and open. Take the direct approach when you ask for help. Tell your colleague what it is you need them to do, and why. Avoid:

- Dropping hints
- Being manipulative
- Flirting
- Acting like a needy, wheedling child
- Ordering
- Bullying
- Calling in favours
- Calling in friendships

◆ Be specific. Tell the person exactly what it is you want and how it should be done.

◆ Negotiate if necessary.

◆ Tell them why the task needs doing.

◆ Tell them what you will consider to be success.

◆ Be honest about the priority level of the task. Not everything can be called 'urgent'.

◆ Give specific deadlines. Never use phrases like: 'Yesterday' or 'asap'.

◆ Tell them at what stages they need to check with you or provide feedback.

◆ Give them confidence in their ability to do the task.

◆ Supply encouragement and praise.

◆ Organise training, if necessary.

◆ Check their understanding and their buy-in.

So What If It's the Boss?

Delegating upward need not be all sweaty palms and serial apologising. We are into an era of partnering, where the best business relationships are built on mutual goals and teamwork. So why the hell should it be so hard to ask your boss to do something?

Of course, it's a power thing. Bosses tend to ask employees to do things, not the other way round. This is the way of the world and it is a sacred taboo in many companies. I'm all for breaking through boundaries, though. All bosses were children at one time so all of them were used to responding to simple commands. The response is inbred. All you need to do is access the right channels.

Rewarded behaviour is the key. Even primates will learn to do tricks if there is something in it for them. If you're delegating to a boss make sure that:

1. You do nothing either verbally or visually to compromise their status. This is something they will defend to the death.

2. You offer them some temptation or reward. You need to show them that it is in their best interests to do this thing. That it will speed things up, create kudos, make them more attractive to members of the opposite sex, whatever. Think IT skills. How in heaven did anyone get them to start typing and doing their own paperwork? Easy. They bought into the whole 'Be-there-or-be-square' package. Learning to type meant access to the World Wide Web. It came with trendy jargon, which they adore, and another opening to become Master of the Universe. If you want to delegate, then try the 'towards pleasure' route, using jargon and increased power or skill base.

3. If that doesn't work, you could try the 'away from pain' route, ensuring life gets increasingly difficult if they don't hack this job for themselves. The problem with this technique is that it often leads to resentment and possibly a reverse-thrust delegation in your direction if you get sussed. Step 2 is often more successful and has long-lasting consequences.

The Martyr Syndrome

Of course, it could be that you are a work martyr and that you are only happy when you are handling everyone else's workload, purely because you enjoy the suffering and the accompanying self-pity it brings. Maybe you are an adrenaline junkie, or you like to be a loner, or perhaps you just like to feel indispensable and impress others with your effort. It could be that you lack the confidence to get into a delegation dialogue.

I have worked with the 'I'm indispensable' lot many times. They arrive on training courses with their mobiles primed, only switching them off when threatened with torture or – at worst – ritual humiliations. When you eavesdrop on their 'urgent' conversations they normally consist of one of two options:

1. They are handling some piece of organisational nonsense that even a monkey could have coped with, let alone a manager, or:

2. They are talking to their boss as though he/she was a little child.

This type of colluded dependency has all hallmarks of the martyr syndrome. The first type refuses to delegate in case something is done wrongly and the second just loves being a mummy figure, ringing her child/boss regularly to ensure he/she has a clean hankie and has worn a vest.

To delegate to others you need to build trust. You have to grow your own confidence, too, so that you're not sitting on jobs just to give you a sense of security. And you need to allow your boss and colleagues to grow up.

CHAPTER EIGHT

Managing Meetings and Organising Events

- ◆ Know your core objectives.

- ◆ Is it necessary?

- ◆ Set a specific agenda and send copies to all participants.

- ◆ Set start and finish times.

- ◆ Chair it well.

- ◆ Get agreed actions at the end. Who will do it? How will it be done? And by when?

Meetings are – by and large – the greatest Time Bandits of the lot. Some people spend their entire working day lurching from one meeting to another, getting punch-drunk en route. It takes a special type of personality to actively enjoy business meetings. People who do are usually:

1. Very sad, or

2. Very boring, or

3. Very frightened.

The bores like to use meetings as a forum to sound off ad infinitum. The frightened people are usually managers who are painfully aware they lack a job unless their time is actively consumed doing something meaningless. Or they know they should be out there managing, but are too scared to face the people they manage. Meetings keep them out of harm's way.

Getting to the Point

Meetings only work if they have a point. Having a point means being called to achieve something and then achieving it. Nothing is more pointless than having a meeting just for the sake of it. Every meeting should be questioned as they call busy people away from their work. Ensure your meetings work by following this strategy:

Planning

◆ Plan beforehand. Know your objective in having the meeting.

◆ Write an agenda and send it out in advance. Make sure the agenda is clear and specific. Don't just write 'Budgeting' as participants will need to know whether you are reviewing last year's or planning the next. Write a more detailed brief under each subject heading, plus an estimated time for each subject. Agenda checklist:

  • Explain objectives of meeting.
  • Break down into subject matter.
  • Allocate time for each subject.
  • Put start and finish times down.
  • Show who is involved in each objective.
  • Let participants know if full or part attendance is required.

◆ Speak to the participants beforehand. Brief them and get an idea of their views. There's no need for these to emerge first at the meeting itself.

◆ Make sure the atmosphere is right. Avoid stuffy rooms or bad lighting.

- Think twice about offering refreshments. Meetings take longer if you do as people see them as a bit of a break from work.

- Think twice about offering seats. The speediest meetings are held standing up.

- Set a strict start time and a finish time and brief others of both.

- Hold the meeting at a time when people will not want to hang around, i.e. 4.00 pm.

- Start on time, even if you are the only one there.

- Always get someone to chair the meeting.

- And someone else to take minutes.

- And someone else to time-keep.

- Don't include 'Any other business' on the agenda. New subjects should be slotted into the next meeting agenda.

Keep it concise

- Hold different meetings for different thinking styles. Some should be for relatively quick, normal business matters. Future planning and brainstorming should be on a separate agenda. The thinking styles are different and one will inhibit the other.

- Brainstorming is best done alone. When you want creative input ask participants to arrive with brainstormed ideas, rather than getting them in the meeting room.

- If meetings turn into a rough-house, get a facilitator to keep them on course. This can be someone other than the chair, with no participation in the meeting, other than acting as impartial referee.

- Write the core purpose of the meeting on a large sheet of paper and pin it up on the wall. When the conversation moves away from the objective, draw attention to the poster as a reminder.

◆ Whinge meetings can be the most time-expensive. Tell participants they can only come with a problem or a complaint if they also bring a possible solution, too.

Steering

◆ Keep the meeting moving in a forward direction. Avoid input that just moves away from the idea under discussion by putting up one barrier after another. Steer people into coming up with ways to make the idea work, as well.

◆ Ask yourself whether you need everyone there. What if you only have participants who are involved in the project or strategy under discussion? Or how about letting people leave when their particular topic has been covered? Nothing is worse than sitting at a meeting when the topic under discussion has no relevance to you or your job.

◆ Steer the speed of the meeting by using closed questions when necessary.

◆ If meetings traditionally run riot, give each participant ten coloured counters. Tell them to use one every time they want to speak, and point out that when the counters run out, so do their opportunities to take the floor. This makes windbags more time-thoughtful.

◆ Get the chair to point out that, although there is room for discussion of a controversial topic, the objective is for the group to move towards an agreement. Tell them that conflict will slow down that objective.

As participants

◆ If you are a participant, rather than the chair, remember that it is up to all of you to make the meeting successful.

- Make your own points clear, specific, concise and full of positive impact.

- Use everyday speech patterns. Don't become too formal or start using unfamiliar vocabulary.

- Avoid use of jargon unless you know everyone there is acquainted with it.

As chair

- If you are chairing, make sure you close down any sideline conversations or discussions. Be firm about shutting people up if they start talking or whispering among themselves.

- Use body language as well as words to steer the meeting.

- Use constantly scanning eye contact to check understanding, involvement and agreement of every participant.

- Use a flip chart to take minutes as you go along.

- Take action minutes. These clarify:

  - What decisions were made.
  - What actions were agreed (linear and global).
  - Who has committed to making them happen.
  - When they will be done by.

- As each point on the agenda is dealt with, decide who owns it and what action is required. Check agreement. Then close the point by crossing it off the list. Make sure ownership is taken by one individual.

- Set dates and deadlines for actions.

- Sum up at the end.

- Distribute minutes promptly.

- Evaluate the effectiveness of the meeting.

Plan the Room

If you are organising a meeting remember that the correct layout is essential. Most meetings are called to either:

* Give information, or
* Make decisions

Information giving

◆ Participant numbers can be higher than if you are decision-making. Over 15, though, and you will get less individual participation.

◆ Room set-up is best as cabaret, classroom, theatre or U-shaped.

◆ The leader needs to work in an authoritative style.

◆ Preparation and planning are a key priority.

Reaching decisions

◆ Twelve should be the maximum number attending.

◆ Room layout is best boardroom or U-shaped.

◆ The leader needs to use the style of a facilitator or chair.

◆ Open discussion is a key priority.

Closing People Down

Each meeting has its own troublemakers. These Time Bandits can hold proceedings up and need to be dealt with as effectively as possible. They are:

1 The roll-over

They want to refer back to the last meeting at great length, preventing the current one from moving forward.

Action: ask for the points from the last meeting that they want to discuss. Make a list and tell them that the relevant ones will be put on the next agenda. If the points are ones they had an opportunity to raise at the last meeting but didn't, ask why. Make a point of asking for their input on issues raised at the current meeting before you close.

2 The pugilist

This person just likes to get into a fight. They will disagree just for the hell of it, in an attempt to score points.

Action: allow for genuine discussion but don't get into a free-for-all. Remind them of the time limit and ask if they would like their views noted. Then tell them the meeting must move on. The more trivial the topic under discussion, the less time that should be allowed for bun fights.

3 The smug

This person avoids making a comment during the meeting but will voice his/her opinion the minute the thing is over.

Action: keep an eye on them. Invite comment and views regularly. If they say they don't have one, ask why not.

4 The windbag

This person dominates every discussion, airing his or her views freely and at length.

Action: invite a couple of comments, to illustrate fairness, but otherwise ignore signals to talk and invite questions from quieter colleagues. Use closed questions. Ultimately be assertive: 'I think we all now know what Brian's opinion is, can I quickly ask for some input from Trevor on that point?'

5 The trickster

Not really interested in the agenda, but happy to quarrel with other small points of procedure, or to question sources of statistics or relative trivia.

Action: close them down quickly, but without humiliating them. Remind them of the timescale and the urgency of the main objective.

6 The joker

Always ready with a merry quip to lighten the atmosphere, but this can turn into time-consuming jokes and other conversation diverters.

Action: again, allow for a wry smile but point out the need to keep on track.

7 The empathetic

Pays too much attention to smaller details like biscuits, tea, room temperature and small talk about babies and holidays.

Action: close down as above. A good reason for not serving refreshments. Suggest they stay around after the meeting is finished for more personal discussions.

8 Silent but deadly

You need their input but they lack the confidence to speak up.

Action: invite comment in a friendly manner, keeping it quite casual. If this fails, speak to them independently before the meeting and ask what their input is going to be on the topic under discussion. Tell them what you need from them and give them time to prepare. If they still bottle it, go through their points yourself.

9 The latecomer

They will be late for their own funeral. They disrupt a meeting by turning up after it has started and asking what has been said so far.

Action: unless this is the MD, never stop the proceedings when they arrive. A nodded acknowledgement should be all it takes, but keep everyone's focus on the speaker. One way to ensure punctuality is to make the last one to arrive the minute-taker, or some other job no one likes.

10 The lazy chair

This person insists on chairing the meeting but does so badly. He or she either dominates with their own views or sits back and allows a bun fight.

Action: suggest meetings are chaired on a rotational basis and forget to get round to this person again.

Managing Meetings: Hot Tips

- ◆ Ask yourself or your manager whether the meeting is really necessary.

- ◆ Could it be held on the phone or by teleconferencing?

- ◆ Pick a location that is convenient to everyone.

- ◆ Try cancelling a few meetings and see what happens.

- ◆ What is the objective?

- ◆ Create specific goals for discussion. Don't say: 'How can we prevent staff leaving?' say: 'How can we boost staff retention by 20 per cent in the next quarter?'

- ◆ Let participants know they will be expected to contribute to the agenda.

- Be strong on discipline. Consider locking out latecomers; recapping takes precious minutes.

- Consider a seating plan to separate troublemakers or chatty types.

- Check everyone can both hear and see easily.

- Check beforehand that all the equipment needed is there and up and running before people arrive.

- Write things to remember on the hardback part of your meetings folder. It's the bit you're least likely to lose or throw away.

- Plan meetings that last no longer than half an hour, max.

- Ban small talk. Make it an agreement.

- Hold meetings on the hoof. Will you be travelling together? Can you hold your meeting on the train or in the station? (Mainline operator GNER even has meeting rooms complete with phone points and fax machines next to its first class lounges at King's Cross, Leeds, Newcastle and Edinburgh.) In a hotel on the motorway? (Travelodge have workspace lounges and meeting rooms available, plus hot-desk facilities with Internet access and teleconferencing facilities.) On the plane?

- Could the meeting be held via videoconferencing?

Organising Events: Hot Tips

Event organising needs clear thought under pressure, so here is a list of quick checkpoints.

Suiting the venue to the event

- Make sure you know the purpose of the event, and brief your team accordingly.

◆ When you check out the venue, meet the staff. Sales teams are always helpful and friendly but that is no indication of the attitude of the real crew, i.e. the ones who will be serving and hosting on the day.

◆ Check car-parking facilities.

◆ Don't just order equipment, ask to see it. Hotels are notorious for coming up with ancient, wonky facilities that look hideous.

◆ Check the number of toilets available and cleanliness.

◆ Check communal areas, like reception rooms. Are you allowed to put up banners etc.?

◆ Will guests be able find their way from reception via well-positioned, clear signs?

◆ How efficient is the heating/air-conditioning? Don't just check on the day, think of your needs on the day of the conference; the venue may be booked in the winter for a conference to be held in July.

◆ Ask for cancellation arrangements.

◆ Check ceiling height and lighting. Lights should be easy on the eye. Low ceilings will prove claustrophobic.

Planning the details

◆ Use a time planner. Computer software will be best. Some produce Gannt charts. The best is probably Microsoft's Project.

◆ Contact the Association of Exhibition Organisers for a list of members.

◆ From the moment you start, keep a book with all your contact names, addresses and phone numbers. Keep them only in the one book, even the ones you think you might not need. Keep the book with you at all times. Transfer numbers from your own directory into that one book. Make it your bible.

◆ Nominate an admin person to deal with pre-conference delegate queries, like faxing maps or checking timings. Arm them with answers to all the usual suspects, like: menu, bringing a spare guest, travel details, end time and if they can get away earlier, copies of speaker notes, cancellations, etc. Give this person sole authority or you will be getting queries thrown back at you constantly.

◆ Budget. This goes haywire when time is tight. When you're stressed out organising an event it gets harder and harder to keep track of costings, receipts and petty cash. Delegate responsibility to someone with financial experience and the ability to be petty, nit-picking and bloody-minded. If they can negotiate as well, great. Make them keep in constant contact with you, though. Brief them on the budget's bottom line.

◆ Before things start rolling give them a list of all the expected costs, like insurance, equipment hire, speaker fees, plant hire, etc.

◆ Don't forget VAT. It can have a big effect on your cash flow.

◆ Don't forget inflation. Check every costing will be held at the quote received.

◆ Make sure *every* necessary piece of delegate information is on the flier. One company missed out the start time and spent three weeks fielding calls.

Success on the day

◆ Pack an 'emergency kit' to take on the day. Include things like extra handouts, sticky tape and Blu-tack, highlighter pens, masking tape, a stapler, pens, spare music tapes, spare PowerPoint discs, etc.

◆ Have an organisers' office that is manned at all times, so that people know where to go with a problem.

♦ File badges for registration in pre-marked envelopes. Never lay them out on a table, it looks messy. It's easier to flick through envelopes than read through a table full of badges every time. Guests dawdle too, trying to read who else is attending.

♦ Have someone to lead people into a 'fill 'em from the front to the back' system. People always start at the back, otherwise, which leads to latecomers having to tiptoe all the way to the front.

♦ People often order drinks and food willy-nilly at venues and this can scupper your budget. Give the hotel one contact name to OK extra items on the day.

♦ Plan diary time to follow up on leads from the conference or exhibition. If work has been piling up in your absence you might find you never get round to it. Following up leads is one of the key objectives of any conference or exhibition.

♦ Collect details of any good venues throughout the year. Keep a file of the 'approved' ones. There's a lot of competition but few live up to their name. Don't lose track of the ones that do.

CHAPTER NINE

Organising Your Workspace and Travel

'Think first, then act.'

OFFICE ANGELS

Quick Tips

- ◆ Arm yourself with the tools of mass destruction (i.e. clear out).

- ◆ Be obsessive. Once you have tidied you are going to stay tidy.

- ◆ Tidy on the hoof. Learn the new habit of clearing and filing as you go.

- ◆ Keep your desk free of all paperwork, apart from the document you are working on.

- ◆ Use the four-box filing system.

- ◆ Tidy electronic files, too.

- ◆ Make your desk space user-friendly.

Yes, it's gird your loins time at last. You knew you were going to have to do this and you know you'll feel better when it's done. It's only starting the chore that's painful and the real Homer

Simpson-style slobs among you will try to cry off with any or all of the following excuses: 'My desk may look like a tip, but the point is I know where *everything* is' or 'I don't have time to tidy.' Shame on you on both counts. If your desk is a mess you are a dirtbag and an eyesore. Office surroundings should be aesthetically pleasing and they can't be if your desk looks like something scavengers could work off for a week.

The good thing about having a proper tidy is that you:

1. Have more space.

2. Can work smarter and faster because you have no junk to slow you down.

3. Look better.

4. Find people make the assumption that your work is as efficient as your desk looks.

5. Smell better.

6. Feel smug and virtuous.

There's no getting away from it, tidying is cathartic. It is good for the soul. It turns you from a demotivated slacker into a lean, mean, fighting machine.

What You Will Need

♦ At least one large plastic bin-bag, maybe two.

♦ At least one hour.

♦ A duster.

♦ Some empty files.

♦ Some empty magazine holders.

♦ Resolve and patience.

♦ A reward.

146   MORE TIME, LESS STRESS

Don't Wait for the Right Mood – Do It Now

Your mood will be all-important to the success of this task, but that shouldn't be used as an excuse for putting it off. Tidying is not for the faint-hearted ditherer. It takes resolve, especially when it comes to binning the rubbish. You are going to have to be brutal. There will be no time for regrets, what's trashed stays trashed. (Tip for the terminally anxious: keep the trashed stuff for one month. If you haven't been sent scurrying to retrieve something from it by then, present it to the bin-man.)

Get Mad

It's good if you can get angry with all your junk. Hate it for messing up your otherwise streamlined life. Curse it for lying there, laughing at you. It is taking the mickey, having a laugh. It shows lack of respect for you. You need to teach it a lesson. It deserves a good whacking. (I've discovered that gangster jargon is often a helpful inner dialogue when dealing with self-motivation in the workplace. Just think *Lock, Stock and Two Smoking Barrels*. Never externalise, though. Calling your boss a slag and a nonce may cause conflict.)

Big Bins

This is going to be the mother of all tidies, too. This is not the 'clear desk' stuff you do every night, when you open a drawer and chuck all your junk in it and retrieve it all the next morning. This tidy is going to get you streamlined.

You may have to get in early to do this one, because the best time to do it is when there's no one else around. This is important for two reasons:

1. Lack of interruptions. You can't work on a desk and give it The Big Tidy at the same time.

2. Image. People should never see you doing anything self-improving. The big thing about self-improvements is that colleagues should never know how you did it. Also they should not be privy to the sight of your rancid old trainers getting retrieved from behind the radiator.

Start With the Easy Stuff

Cast your eye about. If you are a genuine slob there will be things on your desk that are begging to be binned. Take your plastic bag and start with these. I am talking about the empty coffee cups and bent paperclips, or the ageing Post-its and business cards from people who you have long forgotten.

Become Obsessive

You know those people who are forever tidying and plumping up cushions? That is going to be your attitude to your desk – once tidied you are going to guard it like a lion. You are going to be hard on yourself, too. You will make yourself tidy as you go along. By the time I'm finished with you, you will be tidying stuff before you've finished with it. Compulsive tidiers even eschew waste-baskets, preferring a plastic bin-bag or carrier bag close to the desk, which can be disposed of at regular intervals. That's how fussy you are going to get.

Also

While you work at tidying your desk you are going to become obsessive about three other areas, too, namely:

1. Your car

2. Your wardrobe

3. Your bag.

Tidy up your car. Sort out every nook that is harbouring junk. Do the same with your wardrobe. Slimline it. Trash stuff that is style-free or out of date. Then set about your bag or briefcase. Women harbour all sorts of horrors in the nether regions of their hand-bags. My worst-case experience came in the Louis Vuitton shop in Bond Street. The handle on my shoulder purse had broken and I asked them to fix a new one. They said the bag needed to be empty. The assistant gave me a carrier bag and watched, poker-faced, as I emptied what is not much larger than your average man's wallet. The carrier bag was nearly full when I'd finished. The most embarrassing things were the old tissues and free-range Tic-tacs. I don't even know how they got there. The assistant complimented me for getting so much into the purse. And I am quite a tidy person.

The Paperless Office

At this point it is important that you don't waste time ranting about the 'So-called paperless office'. We all know this one was a bit of a con. I won't rant on here, so neither should you. GET ON WITH YOUR TIDYING.

Filing

Every sane person hates filing. Perhaps the worst aspect is delving into old files and rediscovering those documents that haven't seen the light of day for months, but which never seem to be candidates for eviction. If you work in the legal profession or department you may need to be careful about ditching old documents.

But If You Don't Do It?

We all know the penalties of sloppy filing. You can't find things. You spend ages looking. You use up too much space. You get stressed. You get angry. Every job takes longer. You don't dump stuff. You have to read your way through acres of dross to find anything useful. Your colleagues think your work will be chaotic because they tend to judge by what they see.

So, divide your files into three categories:

1. Things I want now

2. Things I need in future

3. Things I need for reference.

Keep files in category 1 close to your desk. But still file the papers involved. Put them away, even for relatively short pauses. This will be a good new habit to create. Keeping short-order stuff sitting on your desk during brief pauses will lead to it still being out there for relatively long spaces of time, i.e. until it is lost beneath the mountain of newer short-order stuff that arrives. Which means you are working in chaos again. File it.

Category 2 files can sit a distance away or be less easy to reach.

Category 3 files will need to be available as and when. This means you get to decide how high the shelf, according to regular, urgent or non-urgent usage. Some of the books or documents may need to gather dust because they're only there for rare but nevertheless necessary usage. Others, like dictionaries, might never gather a speck of dust because you pore over them constantly.

Then:

◆ File as you go. Don't let documents pile up. Filing on the hoof is going to be one of your good new habits.

◆ File in a way that speaks to you, but remember it may also have to speak to a colleague while you are away on holiday or off sick. Don't think scatty, eccentric filing methods will mean you have a job for life.

◆ Don't file anything you can access easily by some other route. This is just keeping extra paper for the sake of it.

- If you haven't found it useful don't file it, bin it.

- Keep a library system next to your filing cabinet to ensure files don't go on long-term walkabout. Make a note of Who? When? and Until? and encourage visiting browsers and borrowers to use this system voluntarily in your absence.

- Don't keep paper copies of things filed in your computer, unless legally required to.

- Colour-code filing for speedy identification.

- If your PA or secretary files for you, make sure you know how the system works too.

- File on a loop. When you file something for 'December 2002' retrieve 'December 2001' at the same time and throw it away.

- Deal with paper immediately or throw it away.

- Create your own system. There is no 'one-size-fits-all' system for filing. Unless you have to do it to corporate standards that is.

- Know what to file, what to pass on and what to bin.

- Use the same system for electronic filing: discard, delete, file or pass on. Don't leave junk lying about.

- Get rid of current files when they run past their sell-by date.

- Remember: 80 per cent of what is filed is never used again.

Make it a goal to keep paperwork off your desk altogether. Valuable desk space should never be seen as an in-tray. In-trays work better on the floor. Your desk is your workspace. It is your home and your territory. Paperwork and other junk, like coffee cups, just eat up that territory.

Paperwork on the desk also dilutes the clarity of your thinking and focus. The eye idles over written words, reading and speculating. You want no distractions when you are working. Your desk needs to be a lean, mean, fighting machine. Get clearing.

Computer Filing

It depresses me how untidy electronic files can get. They are the same as paper files: prune, discard and tidy on a regular basis. Your PC will allow you to file from various sources, like file creation, scanning a document, saving e-mails and downloading from the net. This means flexibility and ease of access, but it also means added and unlimited potential for storing old junk.

Search facilities makes it easy to access even a well-buried or obscure file, but you don't want to spend time running a search every time you need to access something. Keep your computer files stored in a way that is logical and speedy. Pick file names that will mean something to you. Hunting through the wrong files is time wasting. Put as much detail down as you think you'll need when naming the files. Older systems before Windows 95 may have limited you to eight characters, but more recent ones don't.

Back-up

Make sure you back up all your created files, in case the system crashes. Use software like Windows Backup to keep track of key documents so that they can be backed up in one quick operation, without having to identify them anew each time. Never back up on to the same hard drive that holds the original files. Some Internet sites offer secure storage space, or you can use CD-ROM or even floppy disk.

In-trays

You are going to work on the four-box filing system for instant paperwork. This has been mentioned previously, (see page 121), but I will describe it again here to save you time hunting. Quite simply you chuck all new paperwork into one of four boxes:

1. Urgent and important

2. Important, not urgent

3. Urgent, not important

4. Not important, not urgent.

Keep Post-it notes handy as you start chucking the paperwork into one of the four boxes. Write actions (like reply next Tuesday) on to each bit of paper on coloured Post-its as you go along. This should create what is called the one-touch system of paperwork. Each sheet gets identified, actioned and filed straight away. If you go to it again (OK, so maybe *two* touches for some sheets, then) you know *what* to do with it and *when*. This system helps. It works. It is relatively easy.

Shelves

I'm always amazed at the amount of people who stick things they need regularly way out of easy reach. You have desk, floor, drawers and shelves. You probably have high shelves and low shelves. You have shelves that are out of reach. Prioritise items for the shelving and put them in the most appropriate spot, depending on accessibility. Shelves are good for anything in current use or for storage. The trouble with shelves is that they only really store hardback books well. Buy stacks of upright plastic magazine holders for things that go floppy or slithery on shelves, like:

+ Magazines
+ Files
+ Phone books
+ Soft-back manuals

When you are storing magazines for reference, be brutal about only keeping the bits you need. When you skim-read the things first time, use a highlighter pen to pick out subjects or information that you may need later. Or cut out useful articles or quotes and file them. Then bin the rest of the magazine.

Use colour-coding for your paper files, so that you can begin to select at a glance. Theme-file them, if possible.

Bring Forward Files

If you are keeping something in August that needs action in October, put it in the October file, with a coloured sticker telling you what that action is and when it needs doing.

Printed Stickers

I know e-mails are speedy but sometimes it's just not worth logging on and you're too busy to type. Keep some printed compliments slips with a message telling the recipient that you hand-wrote the enclosed for speed of reply. Then try using a pen and paper.

Incoming letters that need an urgent reply could also be written on. Write your comments or reply in the gap at the top or bottom and return it with one of the compliment slips.

Letters

Posting letters is still viable, especially for legal documents or more formal communications. I like letters anyway. They always seem more important. If you use the post regularly, get a complete update of the different way of posting and relevant timings and costings. Deferred post should be done straight away and filed with a Post-it telling you when it needs to be sent.

Avoiding Future Junk

♦ Don't hand business cards out willy-nilly, especially at exhibitions. They are usually kept for use on mailing lists.

♦ Always tick the box offering no further circulars on order forms.

♦ Avoid sending out time-wasting memos, e-mails and letters yourself. Ask yourself if a call will do. Keep communication down to an absolute minimum, which will invite others to do likewise.

♦ Watch out for your own quiet times. This is often when we start to get a bit frisky with our own missives. You begin to send the stuff that isn't important, and to get wordier, because you're bored. You start to gossip or socialise by e-mail. Then you find you can't turn off the incoming mail when your day starts to pick up. Be communication-disciplined at all times. I once moaned about a client who always kept me on the line for a long chat when he phoned. I discovered he thought the same about me. We had both started to ring one another during boring moments at work and those moments were not compatible.

♦ Ask to be kept off internal circular lists if the subject matter doesn't involve you.

♦ Get your PA or secretary (if you have one) to screen your post for you.

So, to sum up:

Be brutal about your paperwork.

Create a strategy and run with it. Do it with every sheet that passes through your hands. You can:

♦ Deal with it immediately, actioning the points or returning it with a reply.

- ◆ Throw it in the four-box system for delayed but speedy action.

- ◆ File it for future use or reference.

- ◆ Pass it on.

- ◆ Bin it.

This routine needs to be non-negotiable. It is speedy to run with and yet it will save you hours hunting through piles of papers on a groaning desk. The time it will save you in terms of distractions and undiluted focus is incalculable. You will think smarter and faster if your desk is tidy. Whittle it down then re-whittle. Be a desk minimalist.

Other Organising Tools

1 The 'To-do' list

This is a long-term favourite, although some people refer to it as though it were the very spawn of the devil. You need to create lists of tasks on a daily basis. This is the time where you prioritise and create order. Spend at least ten minutes at the start and end of every day on your lists, planning and reviewing.

If a job pops up during the day there's no need for you to miss out on that wonderful warm feeling of achievement as you plant a smug tick against it on your 'to-do' list. Simply add it anyway, as a kind of 'dunnit' and tick it as well. Ticks are very rewarding. I don't want you to feel cheated.

2 Personal organisers

I have an inborn horror of anything with the word 'organiser' written into its description. I'm always reminded of those horrible 'organiser' bags in the small ads of colour supplements, with sleeves and pockets for just about everything. A friend succumbed once but spent so long rooting through 1,001 pockets just to find a comb that he binned it eventually. The condom pocket was especially revolting. Imagine lying there waiting while your man roots through his 30-odd organiser sleeves.

The Filofax has a place in history, though, and – for some – has never been bettered. To my memory they started small and then grew. I was particularly impressed with one the other day that was the size of the average Victorian family Bible. They have inserts for everything and the only tragedy that seemed to occur on a depressingly regular basis was that they would get lost. When you rang the victim's phone you would always be greeted with the sorry message: 'I have lost my Filofax with all my phone numbers in it. Please leave your number, plus those of any of my friends you might know.'

3 Paper diaries

You know how these work so I won't waste time here telling you.

4 Personal information managers

You pick your PC package, or it comes with your office software, and it provides you with services like an appointments scheduler, and address book, 'to-do' lists and a time and expenses tracker.

Companies tend to employ these for shared diary information, which is fine until admin add appointments at the last minute and forget to tell you or you forget to add that important little funeral and end up double-booked.

5 Pocket or palm organisers

These can vary from a basic address book to a mini-PC that comes with e-mail and Internet access. If your PalmPilot is compatible to your desktop PC you will find it a useful tool in time management. They are a portable tool, even though the tiny keyboards mean they wouldn't be useful for long document work.

6 Organised space

Give your workspace, no matter how large or cramped, a regular MOT. Everything around you should be in a convenient location and your bodily movement shouldn't be restricted for normal functions.

You should be comfortably seated and your posture not impaired by the level of your PC screen or the inaccessibility of commonly used objects around you. The best way to spot problem areas would be to video yourself working at your desk for three hours and then play it back, speeding the action up via fast-forward. This would provide an excellent movements log.

Once you have tidied your desk, get to work on the objects that are left on it. Get rid of ornaments that cause clutter. You need every inch of spare space for your own freedom of movement.

◆ Is your phone on the correct side? If you write with your right hand it should be on the left side of your desk, so that you have your writing hand free for messages.

◆ Is your mouse in a spot that you can reach easily and does it have enough room to manoeuvre?

◆ Are your feet and legs left with space to move and stretch or do you have clutter under your desk space?

◆ Is your screen at the right height and angle? The top of the screen should be at eye level, or slightly lower.

◆ Keep your arms raised slightly as you use the keyboard and never allow them to rest on the desk edge. You should sit straight at your keyboard so that it is at the same angle as your forearms.

◆ Rest your eyes from the screen regularly.

◆ Use an anti-glare filter.

◆ Move around regularly.

◆ Check things work, if not, bin them. Never hoard redundant pens. You can spend minutes trying to get them to write before placing them back in the pot on your desk again, ready for a repeat performance.

Your Chair

◆ Adjust the seat height so that your legs are not dangling free, or your thighs raised from the seat.

◆ Never use a seat where the height adjuster is broken or the chair has a wobble.

◆ Use a chair that has castors for general adjustment as you move around your desk.

◆ Check the backrest is adjustable and in the right place to support your back. Ideally it should fit into the hollow of your back.

◆ The seat should be long enough to support your legs but not too long. Allow about 5 cm (2 inches) clearance between the front edge and your calves.

◆ Your legs should fit easily below your desk.

Organisation: Hot Tips

Paperwork

◆ Estimate a time for each job before you do it.

◆ Focus and time-lock! Give each job total focus and only handle one job at a time.

◆ 'Double-bag' i.e. do two things at once only if one is boring. For instance, you can double-bag by listening to self-improvement tapes while you are driving. This is also known as multitasking.

- Keep a time log. Do it for two weeks and do it as you go along.

- Inspect your time log for areas of leakage and areas of priority that are time under-funded.

- Do a reverse time log now and again. Think about the week that has gone. If you were given that week again, how would you reallocate or redesign your time?

- Don't over-plan. You can't control your entire day. Allow a little slack.

- Focus on one task at a time. Call this 'focusing and time-locking'.

- Keep your mind in the present. Try not to dawdle around too much in the past, and try to choreograph trips to the future, especially if they're entitled: 'What if?' or 'I'm worrying about what might happen'.

- List jobs in order of priority.

- Don't believe leaving a job unfinished by the end of the day or week is a hanging offence.

- But do finish off when possible, within your work hours.

- Measure your workload so that you know what 'finished' means. Many jobs are, by their nature, endless. You could work 24 hours and never have a feeling of having completed them unless you create your own finishing line.

- Don't react to every piece of paper as though it were an emergency. Set times of the day for going through them.

- Don't postpone the jobs that you hate. Get them done and then reward yourself.

- Never fill your entire day. Plan time for breaks and thinking. If you fear gaps in your diary, invent a name like 'Stuart' and book appointments with him on a regular basis. Other colleagues will respect this booked time instead of filling the gaps in your diary for you.

Communications

♦ Cut down your e-mail output and start a company-wide campaign for other employees to do the same. 'In-box tyranny' is a serious issue in business. The average British working day consists of over twenty e-mails. Research suggests we will shortly be spending about four hours a day handling e-mails.

♦ Do the same with phone calls. We handle around 46 per day, on average. Ask yourself whether both calls and e-mails are really necessary. Ease of communication shouldn't mean an increase in the unnecessary junk.

♦ Set aside times of the day to make phone calls.

♦ Stick frequently used numbers on a personal noticeboard beside your desk or key them into your phone's memory.

♦ Get your secretary or receptionist to screen calls for you. This is more useful than voicemail.

♦ Don't treat e-mail as an immediate communication, like the telephone.

♦ Use Outlook Express's search facility to look up e-mail addresses, and to store others' addresses automatically after correspondence.

♦ Be brutal about deleting e-mails unread if you think they are of no use to you. Know how to spot spam.

♦ When you e-mail someone tell them if you don't expect an answer. The 'thanks' and 'that's OK's can run back and forth for ever.

◆ Postpone incoming calls, even after you've answered. Feel free to tell the caller you need time to think, come to a decision or get further information.

◆ Think of a call as a meeting. Book a time when it is convenient or ask before launching into a long chat.

◆ Keep a timer by the phone and time all your calls. Estimate the desired length of the call before you start talking. This sense of a deadline should make your calls more concise and effective.

◆ If you are putting someone on hold, always ask if they would prefer to be called back.

◆ Stand up, to speed up your calls.

◆ If you work in an open-plan office and get people lurking around your desk waiting to speak to you while you are on the phone, keep a series of written notices handy, with phrases like 'Please hang on, I won't be long' or 'I'll get back to you when I've finished', and point to the appropriate signal, to save wasting both of your time.

◆ Always update voicemail messages, telling callers what the current date is and when you will be back in the office. Some people have messages that are up to a week out of date.

◆ Be specific in your message. Tell callers when you will have 'call-back' time during the day. Give them an alternative for urgent messages, if necessary.

Dealing with people

◆ Set up blocks of time when you will be available to visitors. If people want to interrupt your work to chat, steer them towards these times.

◆ Create weekly planning lists as well as your daily 'to-do' list.

◆ Don't like to be liked too much. If you are known as a good listener to personal problems you will find yourself being interrupted by colleagues on a regular basis. Be there for people when the going gets really tough but become less good at the skill of giving sympathy when it comes to the serial moaners.

◆ Avoid meeting people in your own office. It means you get trapped and have to wait for them to leave. Go to other people's offices to talk instead which keeps you in control of the time. See sales people in reception to speed up cold calls.

◆ Greet people standing when they do enter your office. That way you don't even have to offer them a seat.

◆ Get your PA to interrupt you. Not exactly novel, but still effective.

Getting the best out of your time

◆ 'Double-bag' some of your activities. Combine some of your low-level attention ones, like working out in the gym, with some requiring more focus or socialising. You could meet friends in the gym to work out together, or listen to taped books or business info on headphones as you work out.

◆ Play training tapes or self-improvement tapes in the car as you drive into work. This might also help you avoid 'road rage'.

◆ If you feel your 'fizz' is dwindling, make yourself watch the film *Wall Street*. This shows the speed the yuppies of the 1980s worked at. OK, so most of them burnt out young on a diet of champagne and coke, but it gives you some idea of how fast you can work, if you want.

◆ If a job seems too large to handle, just get started. Small steps get there. Worrying about the whole thing doesn't. Remember the old saying: how do you eat an elephant? Answer: one mouthful at a time.

Expenses

◆ Keep two metal desk spikes for your expense receipts, one for cash and one for cheque or credit card. Spear them as you get them. This keeps them neatly in the correct order.

◆ Write lists of daily expenses down in a paper diary as soon as you get back in the office.

Keeping the pace up

◆ Avoid random, stream-of-consciousness conversations with colleagues during the working day. If a thought occurs to you, write it down to discuss at an agreed time.

◆ If you are doing some fast-paced, urgent work on your PC, arrange for an annoying screen-saver to pop up at shorter intervals than normal. You will keep working just to keep it off your screen.

◆ Avoid 'hypnotic' screensavers. You can waste hours per week just sitting gazing at the more fascinating ones.

◆ Never slump in your seat. The brain slumps when your body does and the posture will reflect in your vocal tone when you speak on the phone.

◆ Use highlighter pens to pick out bits of letters or documents that are useful to you.

◆ Keep a small working library in your office. Buy one good dictionary, a thesaurus (computer ones are never as good as the paper version), a book of business and social etiquette, plus any reference books that will be constantly useful. Don't mix these with your self-help business books. They need longer-term commitment to read.

◆ If you want to go for a break, carry documents. This will make people think you are still working.

Organising Your Business Travel: Hot Tips

Business travel survival depends on pre-planning and paring down. I spend half a week on the hoof. Here are some vital tips:

Packing

◆ Pack as little as possible, especially shoes.

◆ Buy a pull-along case but still check its weight – you will have to lift it more times than you think.

◆ Only buy cases that are lightweight when they are empty.

◆ If you need to carry clothing, use a nylon zip-up suit carrier, not the fold-over leather all-in-ones. These get too heavy and are more likely to cause creasing.

◆ Buy a washable suit from M & S.

◆ Pack underwear between the folds of clothes to prevent creasing.

◆ Buy newspapers and magazines prior to your journey, not at the terminus.

◆ Phone the hotel and ask about availability of hairdryers, fax facilities, etc. Never assume anything, especially if someone else has made the booking for you.

Travelling

◆ Let your PA book everything, but ask for a list of contact numbers if anything goes wrong, from a no-show minicab to stolen traveller's cheques.

◆ Check out the weather conditions in the country you're visiting, plus business cultural dress codes.

◆ Take plenty of business cards when you're travelling abroad – in some countries they are distributed by the ton.

♦ Work your diary so that you can travel to a venue the day before. Do some sightseeing then relax in your hotel room. Travelling via tight deadlines leaves you disorientated. Treat these small breaks as a mini-holiday. If your company insists on sending you off long haul they should at least allow you time to be a tourist as well.

♦ Eat a pre-flight meal that is rich in carbohydrates, drink plenty of water and lay off the alcohol.

♦ Stretch and move around on long-haul flights or journeys. Or do callisthenics in your seat.

♦ Use travel time as thinking, planning and meditation time. Rest your mind and try to avoid any working.

♦ Never travel in your work suit. Change when you get there.

♦ Freshen up using deo-wipes and a light, refreshing cologne.

♦ Use pulse-point aromatherapy sticks to keep you calm while travelling.

♦ One glass of wine while flying equals two to three on the ground.

♦ Jet-lag symptoms can include: disorientation, tiredness, irritability, insomnia and dehydration.

♦ Do stretching exercises on the plane.

♦ Write action notes from a meeting with someone on the back of their business card – only don't do it while they can see you as it can cause offence.

At the hotel

♦ Unmake the hotel bed. There's nothing worse than rolling into it tired after a hard day and finding the sheets have been folded in so tight they feel as though they're nailed to the underblanket.

◆ Carry a brief checklist for your hotel room. Find out where everything is you might need, including the remote control, air-conditioning or heating controls, iron, room-service menu and the spare pillows. You don't want to spend your evening ringing reception to ask.

◆ Use the quick check-out facility. It can save many minutes in the morning.

◆ Take your luggage up to your room yourself. It's only in very expensive hotels that it arrives there before you do.

◆ Never unpack into drawers. Work from your suitcase.

◆ Always ask reception for an upgrade when you arrive.

◆ Be nice to hotel staff. Bad behaviour from guests tends to get its own (often unseen) reward.

◆ If your name is difficult to spell or pronounce, present reception with a business card when you check in. It saves minutes waiting while they trawl through their bookings.

◆ Buy small, lightweight plastic bottles for your beauty and grooming products.

◆ Hang crumpled clothes up in the bathroom and steam by running the hot shower.

◆ Take your own travel alarm clock – it's more reliable than asking the hotel for a wake-up call, and you can use it to time presentations.

◆ Keep the free hotel sewing kits. Put one in every bag.

CHAPTER TEN

Managing Your Technology

┌─ *Quick Tips* ─────────────────

- ◆ Don't let your PC create more work for you.

- ◆ Evaluate every aspect of its functions via time invested v time saved in the long run.

- ◆ Avoid futzing (see p. 169).

- ◆ Get rid of spam.

- ◆ Learn to surf speedily.

- ◆ Don't take chances with new tools; survey their time-saving capacity before you invest.

The first rule in IT time management is: don't treat your computer with too much respect. It is a tool that is there to help you. It should never be allowed to create more work, or to dominate your time. Treat it with as much dignity as you would the vacuum cleaner.

Wasting Time With It

Two problems with IT time management:

1. The Hole in the Sand culture.

2. The fact that, for many people – the computer seems to have filled a gap in their lives. This was the gap that was normally reserved for any or all of the following:

- Partner
- Friends
- Pets
- Life

This is where the vacuum cleaner and the PC start to part company. Nobody that I know would take their vacuum cleaner to bed with them (at least, I *think* nobody I know would . . .). Yet I do know people who sit in bed working on their laptops. Never before has toy, tool and social life blended into the one object. And this blend proves its greatest weakness in time-management terms.

- You can surf the net for research or information, which is time saving.
  But: you can then waste time browsing and generally faffing around. It's a bit like picking up a medical dictionary to study your symptoms. When did you ever manage to put it down after that? How long did you then spend mulling over obscure diseases and ailments?

- You can send e-mails, which is quicker than letter or phone.
  But: you can both send and receive acres of time-wasting junk. (Tips to get rid of spam, or junk e-mail: avoid posting your e-mail address on websites; never pass chain e-mails on – others will reciprocate; minimise your use of webmail; set up your e-mail programme's filters to delete mail from known spam addresses.)

- You can do time logs, diaries, spreadsheets and business plans, etc. and accounts on the screen, which is quicker.
  But: you can take ages learning how to use them and take longer accessing them than you would take working on paper documents.

So, before you embark on any new IT adventure make sure it:

◆ Will save you time. Time invested learning how to use it needs to be offset many times over by the time saved when you can.

◆ Will make your life easier.

◆ Will not be rendered redundant in a matter of weeks.

Reasons *not* to embark on any IT adventures when you are wanting to time-manage:

◆ It is the latest thing.

◆ It looks cool.

◆ It is lots of fun.

◆ My chums all have it.

◆ They try to humiliate me for not having it, as in: 'I can't believe you're not on it! How do you manage?'

◆ Everybody says I will not know how I did without it once I have it.

Be especially suspicious of the last phrase. It has been said to me many times: 'You won't know how you managed without it once you have it.' What they usually mean is: this bastard is a millstone around my neck and I need to see you suffer too.

There are better reasons for using something than this mysterious and clubby-sounding phrase.

Futzing

According to a recent survey, employees spend up to 20 per cent of their office hours futzing, i.e. loitering around chatrooms and surfing sites. OK, so most technology has been invented to add speed and efficiency to the working day. But a lot of it also provides temptation for the procrastinators and the plain bone idle.

Up to a third of workers catch up with the latest sports reports or scores during working hours, forming a large posse of what are called 'sports truants'.

Many companies have now banned personal working on the office PC, or introduced limited access, but the time spent in pursuits like booking holidays, shopping, banking and job-hunting can be costing businesses millions per year in lost time. Not all employers take a draconian view of surfing, though, and some even welcome it as an employee perk. They'd rather have you doing your banking from your desk than being out of the office waiting in a queue.

So, be strict about your objectives when you try to cut time via technology. Don't be seduced by quack doctors selling snake oil. If your life is busy you don't want extra toys, you only need systems that will genuinely speed you up. Don't be ashamed to use paper and pen or telephone and letter when it is easier or more appropriate.

Starting From Scratch

Opt for the easiest system that is simple to use. You'll probably want to start with a word processor, e-mail and information manager. Get a printer that offers quality print and speed. Buy a couple of manuals. The ones entitled *The Complete Idiot's Guide to . . .* (Alpha Books) should do the trick. Nerdish types will tell you that your PC will give you all the help you will need, but don't believe them because it speaks in tongues and those tongues never talk your own language.

You will also be told to relax because your PC is resilient. You can play around on it all you like. This is a lie, too. It crashes, it sends up all sorts of *dire* warning messages. You lose files and you delete work. Be careful.

Two tips:

1. Have the numbers of anyone who can help you near at hand.

(Warning: this dependency will stretch friendships to beyond breaking point.)

2. Keep pressing the 'save' button. (This should mean that everything is stored somewhere, even if it's somewhere on the planet Zod.)

Upgrades

The temptation to upgrade comes within the first hour of owning a computer. The pressure to do so will be enormous. Colleagues scoff at your choice. Computer companies try to make you feel like an old warhorse. Only upgrade, though, if:

1. Yours is broken.

2. Yours is too slow.

3. You need to do something yours doesn't do. (Identify that need yourself. It should be along the lines of: 'I wish this thing could manage my credit card accounts for me.' Beware external seductions.)

Unlock Old Habits

If you are an experienced computer user you may need to take a quick course to unlearn some old habits. There may be speedier ways of doing things on your PC but you're still on the plod because you missed out a couple of generations.

Time Advantages of Your PC

◆ Electronic filing (as long as you tidy your files regularly, just like the paper ones).

◆ Spreadsheets (tricky to learn but good for financial or statistical data).

- Word processor (no more Tippex).

- Project management (good for managing complex functions).

- PowerPoint. If you give presentations and use slides, this is your boy. Easy to use, about ten minutes of training should get you up and running and making your own attractive visual aids. Forget the complicated stuff because that looks tasteless anyway. You won't need to learn how to do complex graphics that fly through the air with sound effects. Your visual aids should be clear, concise and to the point. Just doing bullet points on nice backgrounds is easy. So easy you'll find you can modify them en route, if you need to.

- Voice recognition. This is where you speak, rather than tap in your commands and the computer translates it to the screen. I watched a very early prototype of this function and it would only work if there was no traffic noise and its owner spoke like a constipated Dalek. I assume it has been modified since.

- Desktop publishing. Only use this if it saves time and money, otherwise contract out. Some companies produce documents that are stylish and professionally printed. Others churn out stupid-looking graphics that are a complete embarrassment. This probably isn't a job that you were doing yourself before you knew that you could, therefore it is a slightly suspect time-saver.

- Voicemail. This is an owner-, rather than customer-friendly device. Work out whether it really does save you time.

- Videoconferencing. You need a fast Internet connection, a camera, conferencing software and a video capture card. The time saved not travelling around the globe just to attend meetings will be phenomenal. Once this is perfected, in terms of picture quality and participant performance quality, go for it. It needs commitment or it will become an add-on, rather than instead-of. If you aren't sure about the effect on your time, sit down with a calculator and tot up how many hours you spend travelling per year. How much of that time could be saved if all your meetings took place via videoconferencing?

◆ Meetings. Microsoft Outlook will help arrange meetings by checking the availability of attendees, making bookings in their diaries direct, and sending confirmation requests and reminders by e-mail.

◆ Palm-pilots (pocket-sized computers). Add these to laptops and mobiles and your average railway carriage has enough computing power to launch several flights to Mars. There are three main types:

1. Mobile phone. Most now have Wireless Application Protocol (WAP), and include contact lists, e-mail and diary facilities.

2. PDA (personal digital assistant). Earlier models similar to a Filofax. Now, most function as a mini-desktop PC.

3. Notebook. All the power of a desktop.

All make work more nomadic, which should be time-effective. You can work from home or your hotel, and, when you are in the office, you are no longer confined to a desk or room.

Why a PalmPilot?

* Diary and scheduling use
* Address book
* 'To-do' lists
* Memo pad
* Calculator
* Keep track of expenses
* Synchronise with your computer
* Read and respond to e-mail

PalmPilot Tips

- Buy a screen protector to cut out the glare and protect the screen.

- Learn how to reassign the applicator buttons.

- Put the graffiti cheat sheets into the lid, for speedy reference.

- Reset the time if you're travelling.

The Internet

Great, I think, but:

- Watch distractions.

- Watch incorrect information.

- Watch the sheer volume of information available. It is pretty chaotic out there.

Searching

- Plan before you go.

- Know your objective.

- Keep to the track. Don't stray off it or you could be gone for good.

- Get an appropriate search vehicle.

Directories

These are like catalogues. Good if you are working under one subject heading.

Search engines

These trawl the web for you, looking for specific references.

◆ Be as specific as possible when making your request, otherwise you can get swamped with information overload.

◆ Make sure you put phrases in inverted commas, or the search will pick out each word individually, with all its meanings.

◆ Don't get distracted while you work.

◆ Try different search engines. Start with one that has been recommended but shop around if it doesn't suit your needs.

Watch where you go: porn sites are easy to access but firms are introducing usage policies. You could be sacked for downloading obscene material or accessing hardcore at work. One worker apparently got fired after registering 15,000 hits.

> Don't do anything on the net that you wouldn't want other people to know about.

Speeding Up the Internet

◆ Logging on can be slower at different times of the day. Like shopping, find the best times if you can.

◆ Make your search engine your home page.

◆ Use a British search engine if you're after British content.

◆ Try a meta-search engine like 'Ask Jeeves' if you're stuck.

◆ Have a blank home page. The animated bits take time. Go into Tools and click on Internet Options. Click on 'use blank' on the general menu, and click 'apply'.

◆ www.adfilter.com has software that will disable ads, speeding up downloading of a page.

◆ Surf US sites in the morning.

◆ Try broadband technology.

◆ Use bookmarks. These allow you to store the address of any site you visit regularly.

◆ Use keyboard shortcuts.

◆ Turn off the pictures – they will slow you down. Go into the Tools menu, choose the Advanced Option then go into the multimedia section.

◆ Get a web accelerator.

◆ Switch to a faster service provider.

◆ Subscription-based services tend to be faster than the free ones, but not always. Flat-rate Internet Service Providers (ISPs) tempt users to surf more so can be slower at peak times.

◆ Ask your ISP how many modems it has in ratio to the total number of subscribers. If it's more than ten per modem you'll probably have to dial in several times to get a connection.

◆ Consider cable, digital and ADSL for faster access.

◆ Check out the possibility of a higher-speed connection on your phone line.

◆ Free ISPs often make their dosh via technical support lines, which can run up bills of £1 per minute when you want help.

Empowering the Workforce

The future of IT remains hugely time-productive, but that tends to depend on whose time it is that is being saved. Managers now do much more admin work than before, and are expected to have basic typing skills to do so. Companies are moving towards empowering their workforces electronically, freeing up admin-rich departments like Human Resources by putting the onus back into the lap of the employee.

Company intranets provide unique sources of knowledge management. Staff will be able to log on to the intranet and apply direct for services like training, payroll applications, recruitment systems, benefit packages or pensions changes, entering information directly to the benefit suppliers' systems.

IT: Hot Tips

◆ Nearly half the workers questioned in a recent survey said they felt frustrated by the time spent on solving IT problems. Keep all helpline numbers close by at all times.

◆ Keep calm when you are speaking to the helpline. You will absorb less if you are stressed.

◆ Like calling the doctor, rehearse your PC's symptoms before you speak to the helpline or technician.

◆ If they use jargon you don't understand, tell them.

◆ Write instructions down. The brain has difficulty absorbing simple commands when we get desperate.

CHAPTER ELEVEN

Telephone, E-mail and Fax Techniques

Quick Tips

- ◆ Always check you are communicating with the right person.

- ◆ Know what you want to say. Keep any message concise and clear.

- ◆ Check the person is free to listen.

- ◆ Keep a pen by the phone.

- ◆ Learn effective and 'when-to' use of phone, fax and e-mails.

- ◆ Don't abuse your voicemail system.

- ◆ Learn how your company phone system works, e.g. transferring calls etc.

Are your telephones time-savers or time-wasters? In the short term they provide easy, semi-instant access to friends, colleagues and clients. In the long term, though, they dominate our lives, eating up huge chunks of time in the process. If you are in any doubt as to the schizophrenic role of your telephones and their hero and villain status in your life, do a telephone time log for two average working days. Include *all* telephone time, including aborted calls and time left on hold. I guarantee you will be at least medium-size horrified.

Telephone Time Banditry

◆ Accessibility. For some reason that I have yet to fathom completely, the telephone dominates in terms of urgency. Like the scream of a tyrannical child, its demands must be obeyed. *Everyone* appears to agree with this odd rule of etiquette. I have seen waiting customers cut off in their prime as another client – probably sitting in the comfort of their own armchair – queue-jumps via the simple trick of telephoning the salesperson. Phones are quite simply never allowed to go unanswered. In one shop I watched the assistant ignore it while he dealt with a customer, but even the punter got fed up in the end and suggested he go off and answer it. When your phone rings you jump, even if you are busy.

◆ Or you put it on to voicemail. Which is also a major Time Bandit. People switch them on when they pop to the loo. You get the same message whether they are chatting at the next desk or off on a ten-year sabbatical. Sometimes there are clues in the message but rarely enough to give you even the faintest glimmer of a speedy return call. I even heard a colleague berate his wife for being dumb enough to leave a message by telling her that 'You *know* I never bother to listen to my voicemail messages!'

◆ Or you make people wait on hold. This is, in time terms, like an exquisite form of water torture. Six seconds spent 'on hold' feels like six hours in the real world.

◆ Or you make clients go all around the company, repeating their tale of woe to several departments as they get transferred.

◆ Or you don't even know how to transfer a call, so the client either vanishes into the telephone ether or is forced to call back.

♦ Or you have struck a deal with a colleague to inform one another's callers that you are 'in a meeting'.

♦ Or you switch your answerphone on at home, only to be horrified by the number of friends and acquaintances who use the facility as a 'please call me back' service, forcing you to make and pay for an endless number of calls you would not normally have made, or to feel guilty for not returning their call.

♦ Or you allow yourself to be dominated by your mobile.

♦ Or you use it to send unnecessary text messages on a constant basis.

♦ Or you have it permanently stitched to your ear while you are with friends.

How to Make Your Phone Calls a Complete Waste of Time

♦ Speak to the wrong person. Only tell your tale to the person in charge or the decision-maker. Anything else is just chit-chat.

♦ Get stuck into your list of calls during the lunch break, when there is no one there.

♦ Leave messages asking people to call you back but fail to mention you are in meetings all afternoon.

♦ Waffle. Few people manage to be concise communicators on the phone.

♦ Fail to get to the point.

♦ Leave a message that doesn't include your phone number.

♦ Call 1471 to check who has phoned then ring the number back without checking who it is. When a company answers you sound startled because you don't know who called from there.

♦ Phone people from a train and then act surprised when it keeps cutting off.

♦ Fail to have pen and paper by the phone.

♦ Make a call without having relevant information handy.

Forty Time-effective Telephone Strategies

1. Plan and structure your call before you dial.

2. Check you are speaking to the right person before making your point.

3. Check it is convenient for them to listen.

4. Check there are no distractions looming on your horizon.

5. Use small talk at the start but know how to prune it or cut it off when you need to get down to business.

6. Remember you can't be seen. Make your communication audio-friendly. Gestures and facial expressions are invisible, and pauses while you check details on your screen need explanation.

7. Ask closed questions (i.e. ones that lead to a 'yes' or 'no' or one-word answer) to speed up a conversation. This technique is especially useful when you need rapid information. Try the rail information line to see what I mean: 'Which station are you travelling from?' 'What time of day are your travelling?' etc.

8. Have paper and pen and any relevant documents next to the phone.

9. Use your name when you answer.

10. Take clear messages for colleagues – perhaps they will return the favour.

11. 'Headline' your conversation. Announce what you intend talking about at the start of your conversation, e.g. 'I'm ringing about the sales meeting on the 24th'. This will help the listener to be more receptive.

12. Never try to work while you are listening to a caller.

13. Use affirmation noises and reflect major points back to the speaker to confirm listening and clarify understanding.

14. If you don't understand – ask.

15. Check the spelling of names.

16. Write names phonetically to help pronunciation.

17. Vary your tone more. Voices that are flat can be hard to understand.

18. Find out how to use your phone. Most of us only half-know how it works. Check out all the buttons and switches until you are adept at all the functions, as most of them have been incorporated as time-savers.

19. Find out how the firm's system works. Know how to put calls through to another department. Get your receptionist to give you a brief masterclass if you are still in the dark.

20. Never say 'it's me'.

21. Keep all your most-used phone numbers in one place, near the phone.

22. Pin numbers of facilities, like couriers or engineers for printer breakdowns, in front of your desk if possible.

23. If you leave a message on someone's phone asking them to ring back, tell them when you will be available.

24. Make appointments for telephone conversations if your colleague or client has a busy schedule.

25. Leave clues to your whereabouts or availability on your voicemail and give an optional number to speak to someone who can give out information if the call is urgent.

26. Don't eat or drink while you are on the phone.

27. Summarise your major points or agreed actions at the end of the call.

28. Use speed-dial.

29. Leave a personal message on your mobile, so that callers know they've got the right number.

30. Tempting though it may be to tape music and jokes, keep your answering message brief. Callers are paying to listen to your ego trip.

31. If you keep getting wrong number calls try to discover the number they should be ringing. I kept getting calls for the local council and it became quicker to give out the right number straight away.

32. Try to create a quiet time each day when you can sit with a phone making outgoing calls without interruptions. First thing in the morning is a good time because most people are at their desks then and you can have a good call-cull.

33. If you are doing business with a manager or boss of a company, get to know their PA. Once the main business has been booked, a PA who knows all about your dealings will be speedier to contact than the client him/herself, especially if you are fixing appointments for meetings etc.

34. Stand up to make important calls. It adds tone and clarity to your voice.

35. Never make a call when you are slumped in your seat.

36. Never make a call with your hand over your mouth.

37. Always be a good listener on the phone – sounding bored will make the speaker less confident, resulting in waffle and time-consuming repetition.

38. If you are right-handed, keep your phone on the left side of your desk so that you can write while you are talking.

39. If you take a lot of calls, try to get a hands-free headpiece.

40. Cut callers short with a kitchen timer. When they hear it go off and ask what it is, tell them you *think* it's just the fire alarms being tested.

How Not to Waste Time Spent on Hold

Three alternatives:

1. Refuse to be kept on hold. Ask the other person to call you back. (This technique works best if you are either famous or MD of a multi-million-pound corporation.)

2. Wait but 'double-bag' to occupy the time, i.e. have some other small task ready prepared to do. Avoid anything too complex or you will become absorbed and therefore unprepared when your call finally gets through.

3. Tell the person putting you on hold that you are prepared to wait a few moments, but would they please take your number to call you back if you have to cut off.

Why You Never Have a Pen By the Phone

We tend to make calls in a reactive manner, even the business variety. The first thought is to speak to a person, the rest of the time between that and dialling is employed searching for their number. Which is why we connect unprepared in 80 per cent of cases. The connection startles us. We don't plan either the structure or the content of the call. We lack the tools and the documents. Pessimism makes us suspect the other person will not be available but perversity means we don't even plan our message for the voicemail.

Before each call, then, *plan*. Know:

◆ Your objective.

◆ Your major points.

◆ What information you require from the other person.

◆ The full name of the other person.

◆ Any information you need to supply, like reference numbers.

And have:

◆ Any documents you will need handy.

◆ Any tools, like a pen, you will need handy.

When to Phone and When to Fax or E-mail

Always use the phone or speak face to face when it is any of the following:

• Selling
• Persuading
• Negotiating
• Building a client relationship
• Asking out on a date
• Breaking bad news
• Sending condolences
• Congratulating
• Sacking
• Divorcing (according to statistics, one in ten women ditch their lovers via computer)

Use the fax when you:

* Want a printed record
* Send diagrams
* Send maps
* Want to write a letter but don't have the time

Use e-mail when you:

* Want to send a very speedy, concise message
* Want to send a quick copy of something written
* Want to be funny
* Want to splatter-gun several people with your copy

How to Take Messages

◆ Take messages for a colleague with a good grace. Be polite and helpful.

◆ Use a proper message pad.

◆ List:

  * Caller's name
  * His/her job title
  * Department
  * Phone number
  * Time of call
  * Action or message
  * Your name for reference

E-mail

Now that 18.9 million Britons are on-line, e-mails are the new letter. Most Brits under the age of 25 have never even written a formal letter, but the e-mail, that speediest form of correspondence, can waste vast acres of work time by their sheer volume alone. Add to that the fact that many are poorly composed and therefore ignored or deleted before being read, and you can see why e-mail etiquette can be a useful time-saver.

The big problem with e-mail is its casualness. You can write without thinking. You can dash off notes at the speed of a blink. The trouble is that, for the recipient, reading them takes the same time as reading a letter. Except people send fewer letters because they are so much hassle to compose.

So there is an obvious bottleneck effect with e-mail. Too many are being sent and recipients are feeling under siege. One of the biggest time complaints in business always refers to the amount of e-mails or lotus notes that build up. Urban legends are built around people returning from holidays to find trillions of e-mails waiting unread. And the situation can only get worse as everyone goes on-line.

E-mail pros

◆ Speed of message.

◆ Avoids falling into the voicemail trap.

◆ It can be used 24/7.

◆ It can mobilise people quickly, company-wide.

◆ It cuts down on paper use.

◆ Faster decision taking.

Do

◆ Put your entire subject matter in the subject line. Be as specific as possible. This is one of the most vital parts of your e-mail message. Most people try to decide on a title and then give up, using something non-specific, like 'Hi' or 'Feedback' instead. Let the reader pick out the subject straight away from the list of e-mail titles. This will also let him/her arrange their focus before starting to read your missive.

♦ Be concise and clear. Stick to your main message and don't waffle. One of the Internet's golden rules is: 'Don't make your reader use the scroll bar for important information.'

♦ Sign off correctly. Some people even sign business e-mails 'love and kisses'.

♦ Never send an unnecessary e-mail. Doing so encourages others to do the same.

♦ Check composition and spelling.

♦ Check it goes to the right person.

♦ Check you haven't blasted off a knee-jerk reaction that you might live to regret.

♦ Don't copy to more people than you need to, just because it's easy to do.

♦ If your communication is dragging beyond three or four messages then it's time to get off your bottom and go to speak face to face. E-mail can't produce body language and vocal tone. If it's not working then you need to change the style of communication.

Remember:

♦ Have I spellchecked it?

♦ Is the tone right?

♦ Will I regret it?

♦ Who will read it?

♦ Is it too informal?

♦ Have I spent too long deliberating over the subject line?

♦ Have I used any terms or words in my subject line that spammers use? If so, it might get left unread with the reader assuming it's junk mail.

- Use e-mail to send data and get answers, not as a substitute for conversation.

- Watch net abbreviations. If they're not understood your message has wasted time. Ditto general abbreviations.

- Prune to no more than three paragraphs.

- Practise triage on your received e-mails: urgent? Later? Never?

- Send a stock message, acknowledging receipt, for non-urgent messages.

Communication: Hot Tips

- Write business letters that are concise and clear, in simple English.

- Structure your letters before you start them.

- Keep a dictionary on your desk. Spellcheck is fallible.

- Avoid using clichés. They say little but annoy lots.

- Use active, rather than passive tenses to create impact and increase interest and understanding, e.g. 'We *chose* to go with the original plan', rather than: 'A choice was made . . .'

- Listen first.

- Then understand.

- Then speak.

- Use 'headlining' to alert people in advance to your own subject matter, as in: 'Alan, about that meeting on Friday to discuss the green conference . . .'

- Speak in the other person's language. Look at their pace, style and use of words. Are they emotive or logical? Do they like speed or detail and construction? Do they describe things by feelings, or visually or logically? Do they like facts and figures or excitement? Mirror their overall style to create easier assimilation.

♦ Take a pause before speaking. Does what you say have structure and impact?

♦ Avoid waffle.

♦ Use pauses and silences for impact.

♦ Compliment the other person's viewpoint or create empathy.

♦ If you disagree, be specific, not insulting. Put-downs come from:

   • Implying the speaker is lying
   • Stereotyping
   • Making decisions on their behalf
   • Making assumptions about what they are going to say
   • Using emotive words
   • Being patronising
   • Arguing with their values or beliefs

These are all turn-offs that will slow down the communication process and probably lead to conflict or resentment.

♦ Discuss your feelings but do so without emotion.

♦ Plan to combat barriers to listening. Not listening wastes time. Look at:

   • Language barriers (also caused by accent)
   • Environmental barriers (room too warm, etc.)
   • Psychological barriers (listener is stressed or nervous, etc.)
   • Content (of no apparent interest; heard before; too controversial, etc.)
   • Physiological (tiredness; hearing problem; hunger, etc.)

CHAPTER TWELVE

Leadership and Management

'There are no office hours for leaders.'
CARDINAL JAMES GIBBONS

According to a survey by Office Angels, office workers claim that during the summer-holiday exodus of bosses, colleagues and clients, 'annoying interruptions' are reduced by a third, enabling them to get more work done. So what do staff do when the boss is away?

- ◆ 96 per cent take a full hour for lunch, claiming it made them feel happier and more focused for the afternoon.

- ◆ 35 per cent read newspapers or magazines when the attention drops at 3.00 pm.

- ◆ 44 per cent started talking to themselves.

- ◆ 4 per cent nodded off.

Quick Tips

- ◆ Learn how to lead and how to manage. Most managers play it by ear.

- ◆ Understand how an effective leader is a time-managed leader. It is your job to enable staff to get their jobs done quickly and comfortably.

◆ Train, delegate, motivate and empower.

◆ Be a good communicator. Knowing your vision is not enough – others have to know and understand it, too.

◆ Manage in the IT age.

If you are a leader or a manager – or have aspirations to being either – you need to be aware that you are navigating through the Information Age. Speed is a vital ingredient for corporate survival, and speed requires rapid mobilisation and change. Of all the employees in any company, it is the manager who most needs the ability to work and think fast. Fast means faster and faster. To build or maintain a successful reputation a company needs to be able to move on:

1. Internal communications.

2. External communications.

3. Client demands and expectations.

4. Client 'delight' factors.

5. Updating IT.

6. Marketing.

7. Product development.

8. Supplier demands and relationships.

Being a leader or manager in this age requires:

◆ Action-focused thinking.

◆ Energy.

◆ Creativity.

◆ Effective communication skills.

A degree of impatience is the order of the day. If you sit back satisfied too readily, or are smug or complacent at your own success, or you become too tolerant of delays and red tape, you will be in the same league as an athlete who starts to put on weight. Cumbersome leaders head up cumbersome companies. Watch some of the huge old UK 'institutions' try to turn on a sixpence when the competition begins to bite. And then watch these unwieldy dinosaurs start to head for extinction, like the final scenes in *Jurassic Park*.

Smart managers need energy, not just to deal with the stresses and speed of their own jobs but to inspire and motivate their teams through theirs. Energy and enthusiasm are contagious, but so are cynicism and complacency.

The fast manager keeps few habits. There is no 'right' way of doing things, apart from the best and most effective one. Experience is less of a virtue if it has only led to a suspicion of change and a sense of pre-judgemental mindsets based on historical and non-applicable events. Experience should open the mind, not close it. Learning should be constant.

Some Talents of a Leader in the IT Age

◆ The ability to set specific goals and targets.

◆ The ability to communicate their vision.

◆ Enthusiasm to inspire.

◆ Empathy and communication skills to motivate.

◆ A high profile among the workforce.

◆ A sense of calm.

◆ The ability to think and respond quickly.

◆ Creativity and unfettered thinking.

◆ 'Towards' thinking, focused on objectives, not barriers.

- The ability to hire quick-thinking staff.

- The ability to make mistakes.

- The ability to recognise and reward talent.

- The ability to delegate.

- The ability to listen and understand.

- The ability to ask the right questions.

- The ability to speed processes up and cut through the crap.

- The ability to take risks and be innovative.

Listening

You will need to spend time listening, but not to the wrong people. Bad managers waste time listening to the wrong advice. This is not part of the process of *learning*, it is part of the process of *dithering*. Remember: training and hiring consultants can be a clever way of avoiding putting into practice what you already know.

People to Spend Time Listening To

1 Your employees

They do the job. If you hire the right people they should have the best ideas. Don't make it hard for them to share those ideas with you. Remember staff 'Ideas Boxes'? They were great. Make one up on the e-mail.

People do their best thinking when they're alone. Don't expect great ideas to come at meetings. E-mail is better. Allow your staff to come up with stupid ideas as well as smart-alec ones. This is called being creative. Some of the best ideas sounded stupid to start with.

Do 360-degree appraisals and hear your staff give their ideas about you, too. Think about changing when you hear them, don't always try to justify or argue. Get your managers to go 'back to the floor' and join them as often as possible. You all need to do the job otherwise you'll never understand the true issues. Make your sessions regular and non-negotiable in your diary.

2 Your Customers

Many companies lose touch with their customers which means they are working on assumption, not fact. People buy or use a service for reasons no one man could ever guess at. There is little logic in the way we decide to buy. There is even less in why we choose to 'like' or 'dislike'. Take a look at popular characters currently in vogue. Are they all nice/attractive/talented/sexy/interesting? Very few are any of these. Keep in touch. Expect fluctuations. Never get complacent or smug. Work constantly to improve the service, as well as the product. When I train in customer care I ask the delegates to cite cases where they have received good or exceptional customer care. I rarely get an answer. Customer service is more than just the icing on the cake. In modern business it *is* the cake. Customers are more demanding than ever. Listen to what they are trying to tell you.

The Prêt à Manger chain gives excellent customer service. I asked one of their managers how they get the best out of their staff. I was told it came from three areas:

1. Recruitment. They pick the right type of person, they don't just recruit on skill or experience.

2. They keep their staff happy. Happy staff provide good customer care.

3. Their staff use eye contact. They look at the customer and therefore are observant. They see our needs as they arise.

I would suggest the company is also innovative. They try out new products. They give the customer what he wants before he knows he wants it.

Reward staff according to the response of their customers. This will create a genuinely customer-focused workforce.

Leadership Styles

You can lead a team or even an entire company with a vast range of styles and techniques, all of which may or may not be successful under different circumstances. No one style is 'right', although some may be 'wrong', especially any that involve bullying or harassment.

I was brought up in the autocratic leadership culture. The boss was the boss and everyone knew it. All you looked for were 1,001 ways to sound genuine while agreeing with whatever he said. If you were a favourite you got treated well and if you weren't you got ignored or dumped on. But that was the rag trade in the 1970s and that was pretty much the norm. It was noisy and I liked it. It worked insofar as people got on with their jobs and were motivated primarily through fear, either of being shouted at or being sacked. There was a strange security about it all, as a child feels with a strict parent.

Now most leaders I meet tend to be consultative. They rarely give orders. They discuss and empower. They are appraised along with their staff. Either that, or they are invisible. Either in meetings or travelling the globe, they show their faces so rarely that they are barely recognised when they do. The companies they run are so huge that they are obscured by the mists of their own greatness.

'Cometh the moment, cometh the man' is probably true of most great leaders. When a company rolls along successfully the consultative style works well enough. When there is an emergency then there may be a need for speed and crisis management. People will be told what to do, rather than asked. Consultative processes will need to be cut through. You don't want six people on a committee sitting around deciding which exit to use in the case of a fire.

Five Main Management Styles

1 The enthusiast

Entertaining, fun, creative and often inspirational, this manager likes to be seen by and to communicate with his/her staff. Power is an important factor in the job but he/she will not wield it too strongly. This person is an entrepreneur at heart, coming up with new, innovative and exciting ideas but often lacking the where-withal to carry them through to the bitter end. He/she has a short attention span and needs to work with people who can add substance and detail to ideas and schemes.

2 The driver

This person manages by command. Objective and task-driven, he/she will focus on the job in hand, often at risk of relationships and team dynamics. Their vision is all. They like power and authority and will not suffer fools gladly. They expect commitment from their staff. They talk about empowerment, but don't mean it. They get bored easily, especially with time-wasters and wafflers. A results-freak into new technology and everything cutting-edge.

3 The nurturer

This manager builds a team and encourages them to self-manage. They are a very light hand on the rudder but are there to consult and guide when necessary. Their main focus is the staff and their concerns. They will be into people problems and issues and will keep an open-door policy. They can be long-winded and like to be popular.

4 The strategist

This manager is totally focused on the paperwork of his/her job. It is the facts and figures that interest them and they like logic rather than emotional input. They are forward planners, but with a firm eye on tradition, routines and past experiences. They would not stick their neck out for anything creative or untried.

5 The wheel-hub

This manager can be any or all of the others, depending on what style is needed. He/she can roll with the times, flexing his/her way of managing depending on the team member or the situation of the day.

Time Tips for Managers

◆ Don't let your staff delegate minor stuff to you. They will happily pile all their responsibilities on to your desk.

◆ Watch out how many of their tasks and decisions you pick up. The more you do the more they'll think you want to do.

◆ Empower them to make some of the decisions and take the credit as well as the blame.

◆ Don't be 'open door' all the time. Book periods during the day when you are free to talk and let your team know when these are, but allow them alternative ways of contacting you.

◆ Be high profile.

◆ Effective recruitment is your greatest key to success. Invest time in making sure you get the best staff, then spend time making sure those people are happy and motivated.

◆ Recognise work well done and reward it.

◆ Don't do jobs because you enjoy them. Delegate everything you can.

◆ Check staff leave on time – don't encourage late work.

- Encourage open communication and feedback. Your team shouldn't feel that they have to watch their words in your presence.

- Encourage your team to be customer focused, not 'you' focused. Some large companies run into problems because staff hide problems from the chief executive or MD. It's the customers they should be keeping happy, not you.

- Create a fun environment. People work better if they are enjoying themselves.

- Don't create a faux-fun environment. Some companies employ clowns and fancy dress days to enforce fun on stressed, overworked staff. Don't make them have to pretend.

- Check work conditions are the best. Air, space, colours and lighting are all important. Don't create a battery farm.

- Communicate clearly. Don't leave requests or even orders open to misinterpretation. Poor communications are time-consuming. Brief people well.

- Accept that some communications don't work. It's no good telling staff the information they are asking for has been pinned to the noticeboard for a week. If it's an ineffective form of communication, so be it. Accept that fact, don't argue with it. Change your methods to those that work.

- Don't manage in 'Critical Parent' mode. When you do this you become a 'rescuer', telling people how things should be done until you feel forced to turn round and do them yourself. Once you have moved into 'rescuer' you are inches from becoming 'victim', i.e. the one who ends up doing all the work him/herself. Allow your staff to take on problems. Don't pick them all up yourself. Life is all about problems and how we choose to solve them. If your team's favourite way of solving a problem is to dump it on to you then you are the one with the biggest problem.

♦ Get your team to come to you with problems only if they also bring a solution, too.

♦ Get to know your staff as people, not just as employees.

Strategic Thinking

As a manager you will need to free yourself up from day-to-day tasks to work on the long-term planning. This is a vital part of your time plan. Without an overall strategy your daily tasks are impotent because they are not working towards a goal. If you have future plans then the energy being used in the present will not be wasted.

The Strategic Framework

1. Compiling and analysing the information needed to understand your core problems.

2. Being focused on your USPs (unique selling points) – what are the company's competitive strengths?

3. Defining the scope of your product in the marketplace.

4. Knowing the resources at your disposal and deciding how to capitalise on them.

5. Identifying necessary changes.

6. Communicating your objectives.

7. Implementing changes successfully.

8. Monitoring and, possibly, changing your strategy.

9. Having measurable standards for that success.

10. Motivating your team en route.

Effective strategists look at what is happening now in the context of where they want to go.

◆ Always consider the long-term implications of short-term actions.

◆ Work out a timetable for your strategies. Give yourself deadlines and time goals.

◆ Plan your team according to your overall strategy. Think like a football manager – make changes to the team where and when necessary.

◆ 'Sell' your ideas to your team.

◆ Check understanding and commitment.

◆ Don't just market your ideas emotionally. However strongly you feel about your vision they won't just buy in for no other reason. Back your enthusiasm up with facts and knowledge.

◆ Review your strategies regularly. Circumstances change, often overnight. If your plans cannot cope with change they will snap in two.

◆ Be customer-driven not competitor-driven.

◆ Give people what they want, don't try to make them want what you want to give them.

◆ Use a SWOT analysis regularly:

  ◆ Strengths
  ◆ Weaknesses
  ◆ Opportunities
  ◆ Threats

◆ Make any mission or vision statements unambiguous.

◆ Keep records of every step to use when implementing future projects.

◆ Assess the risks.

◆ Assess the impact of success.

◆ Sew in some back pockets – make contingency plans.

◆ Review each stage.

Dealing With Poor Starters

◆ Try not to dump the entire task on them with one deadline. The enormity of it all will probably cause procrastination. Give it to them in bite-size chunks.

◆ Give them the quickest start time. Delays will only cause dither.

◆ Handle excuses before they arise. Tell them what is not negotiable.

◆ Discuss project stages early on. Then give them freedom to roll once they have got going.

Dealing With Poor Finishers

◆ Temper initial enthusiasm by asking for longer-term project plans with as much detail at the end as the start.

◆ Set deadlines for each stage and brief these fully at the start. Nip any signs of slippage in the bud.

◆ Emphasise overall end time and why it is important.

◆ Don't allow excuses.

◆ Beware of too much praise and enthusiasm at the start of the job. Reward at the end.

◆ Avoid letting them over-promise in case of under-delivery.

Self-motivation

Managers and leaders motivate and praise others, but who motivates and praises you? You need energy and focus to tackle your jobs in good time. When the energy or enthusiasm lags you need to find ways to coach yourself towards time fitness. Negative internal dialogues are your worst enemy, known as 'loser tapes'. When you start to play 'loser tapes' in your head it is vital you turn the dialogues around into positives.

When I am tired I start to suffer from self-pity, and it is then the 'loser tapes' kick in. I undervalue my own potential. I tell myself to give up, that I am 'doing too much'. But when I am feeling up I know I can do all that work and more. My dialogue tries to scupper my objectives. I turn into a wuss. I need to pull myself together. I do it with the help of role models.

Everyone over the age of forty starts to wonder whether they shouldn't start to take it a bit easier. I think of Margaret Thatcher, who was running the country and getting four hours sleep a night and, apparently, thriving. I need to remind myself that my ideal stress levels aren't as high as hers but they are still some way up the scale. When I lack resolve or physical effort I think of Shackleton or Chris Moon, who lost an arm and a leg and still went on to do marathons. It's only me telling myself I can't cut it. My body would probably tell me otherwise.

Tackle yourself. Read about inspirational people. Get a vision of your own potential, which is boundless. Don't be a wuss.

Ethics and Values

Time management may sound like the shortest route from A to B, but it isn't. Task and objective-focused managers can believe that the end justifies the means. If you are prepared to do anything to sell, make a profit and look successful to your shareholders then you may decide to be brutal in your methods. But you may find that, in your rush to become the best in the shortest space of time, you have compromised your own ethics and values.

Now is the time to define those ethics. As a manager you can get the most out of your team, or the best out of your team. You can set unrealistic deadlines and press them until their pips squeak. Or your can focus on having happy and healthy staff with a good quality of life.

Times are changing and companies are looking at the global picture, but by global they aren't just meaning doing business nation to nation via the net, but the repercussions globally of those fast-track services. To make your business faster, cheaper and more competitive, do you want to employ cheap labour from abroad, knowing those workers are underpaid and working in bad conditions? Do you want to see people in your own office leaving at 7.00 pm or 8.00 pm and returning after a miserly couple of hours with their families? Now is the time to sketch out some values, before you get sucked into your strategy planning and time-management techniques.

CHAPTER THIRTEEN

Fast-track Decision-making

┌─ *Quick Tips* ──────────────────────────────────┐

- ◆ Consider decision-making as a process built on strategies.

- ◆ Speed up some of that process by applying a deadline, just as you would do for any other task.

- ◆ Monitor the effectiveness of any decision you do take.

- ◆ Define what you mean when you describe the 'right' decision.

- ◆ Allow for both logic and randomness in your decision-making.

- ◆ Get the factors down on paper.

- ◆ Decide on goals before you decide on the process.

- ◆ Analyse the emotional factors involved.

- ◆ Divide decision-making into a series of stages.

└──┘

Did you ever work out how much time you spend making decisions? Some of the greatest ones can be made frighteningly quickly. I decided to buy a house costing half a million in ten minutes. When I accepted a marriage proposal I went from not even having considered the idea to saying 'yes' in approximately three minutes. I have spent longer deciding whether to have a skinny or full-milk latte in Starbucks. Business decisions come with their own special worry. They affect others. They will blame you if you choose wrongly. They may almost look forward to doing so. Some employees think that is what managers are for: to make decisions and then pick up the blame and the ridicule.

So how to speed up a difficult, complex process like decision-making? Easy. Most decisions can be made in one of three ways:

1. Deciding to do nothing.

2. Deciding to take a decision.

3. Deciding to toss a coin, or let someone else decide for you.

So your first step is to select an option. Don't be too scathing about the coin-tossing option, either. It can be a valuable way to break a mental deadlock. When the side comes down you will immediately feel whether that was the decision you wanted or not. It can be a good way to access your own preferences.

Letting someone else decide for you is only effective if you delegate the decision for sound reasons. If you feel the other person has better knowledge, then fine. If you just want someone to blame if the decision is wrong, then you need to think again.

Deciding not to decide is within the viable options. Some things will heal or go away if allowed the luxury of time. Some problems are better left untouched. But this action should be based on an assertive response, not a passive one.

Authority

Another factor in your speeded decision-making process will be authority. Is the decision yours to make? What is the scope of your power in the situation? Once you have made your decision, can you run with it or are there other factors involved? Will you then have to persuade and influence others to agree? Decisions need ownership to be effective.

Risk

Keep in mind the element of risk involved in any decision. How much risk does your job or your company allow? Draw a line down the middle of a page. Imagine high risk to be to your right and low to your left. The onus of desired risk will affect your decision tremendously. Put a cross on the page to illustrate how much risk you can allow in this particular outcome. This will begin to cut down your options, and already your decision-making has created helpful limits.

Is your work culture innovative or bureaucratic? Is there a predictability and conformity, or is risk part of the system?

Three-part Structure

Now divide your decision-making process into three:

1. Identifying the problem.

2. Taking a creative look at alternative courses of action.

3. Eliminating the alternatives to reach a decision.

Part one will probably include actions like:

◆ Gathering information.

◆ Research.

◆ Asking advice.

This will all enable you to make an informed decision, rather than one that is purely based on 'feel' and assumption.

Part two should include:

- Creative brainstorming.

- Writing options down.

- Sorting the possible from the impossible.

- Being fearless of numerous alternatives, e.g. complexity.

- Keeping an open mind.

- Using 'towards' thinking, as in: 'How can that be done?' rather than 'Why can't that work?'

Part three will include:

- Whittling down according to criteria, feasibilities and weighting.

- Looking at the 'what if' factor, i.e. what would happen if you chose an alternative and implemented it.

- Visualising each outcome.

- Deleting each negative until you produce a positive choice.

Weighting

This technique can help turn assumption into a decision based on logic. If you are deciding to make a purchase and are given several options, write a list of your criteria in order of importance. For instance, a car purchase might be based on:

- Reliability
- Colour
- Cost
- Hatchback
- Low running costs etc.

Once you have your list you can set each car on offer against it, giving it a score, until you reach the ideal to suit your requirements.

Gut reaction

I never dismiss this aspect. Psychologists say that instinct and gut reaction come from rapidly sifted knowledge. That what we consider to be random and emotional has in fact been based on information. It's just that our brains have worked quickly, to produce sleight of hand.

I consider this to be a vital part of the decision-making process, but it should rarely be the *whole* process. Back at least some of it up with solid fact. Psychologists can be wrong. You don't want to fall prey to nothing more than fancy. Your boss might not like it, apart from anything else.

Outcome Analysis

This is another way to plot your decision. Start with your desired outcome. What do you hope your decision will achieve? Ask yourself whether that outcome will present its own problems. Then list your possible alternatives and compare the effects of each.

Committing

You need to work through the 'wavering' stage of decision taking. We like to be firm and committed but we also like the comfort of an 'opt-out' clause. Unfortunately this can scupper the clarity of the decision.

Margaret Thatcher committed herself to 'No U-turns'. This sold strength but it also smacked of inflexibility, which could spell disaster. But don't allow your wavering to become stressful or turn into dithering. There is a stage with any decision where it is necessary to provide commitment. An absence of this will mean you lack the drive to ensure success. Fear of failure can lead to lack of commitment. All you do if you act in a dithering way is to prove your suspicions about a negative conclusion right. Once you have made your decision you need to act with self-belief. Monitor the outcome and be flexible enough to change tactics, but that flexibility should not be driven by lack of resolve. Measure the success of any decision by its results, not by the process alone.

Again: don't sweat the small stuff. Keep your time and skills for the key business decisions. Those that don't matter much should be dealt with rapidly or ignored. Your brain can only cope with so much. Why ponder for minutes over your coffee machine choice each morning? Why hover over the salad selection wondering whether to have green or mixed? Why dither over your print size or the colour of your socks? Some decisions are made better through habit.

Habits

I have always fought against habits. Considered them to be a sign of old age. But then I got busy at work. I can't afford to dither over the small stuff. I have the same coffee, the same sandwich and the same drink in the pub. You might catch me pondering the big problems at my desk but you won't see me sitting in front of the waiter in the wine bar with a furrow in my brow.

Habits help with time management and habits help with stress, unless you become obsessive and then the system starts to break down. I have a favourite seat on the train. If it is free I use it. If someone is sitting there I go to another. If your habits become so fixed that you have a panic attack when they are forced to change, you need to spend some of your precious time on a visit to the psychiatrist.

Procrastination

We all like to put some things off, but bad time-managers delay almost *everything*. Some people are habitually late, often to the point where they will always be ten minutes late for every business appointment. If you are a serial Time Bandit you are responsible for the chaos of everyone's time because one person's lateness will start a ripple effect on the entire schedule of the company. Being regularly late means, in fact, that you are a very *good* time-keeper. You are just running out of synch with your deadlines. You are punctual, but late-punctual, rather than on-time-punctual. In other words, you have no problem with time itself, just a lack of courtesy and respect for the people you deal with. For some reason you are not troubled by the fact that you keep them waiting. You need to catch up. Run to the same schedule, only set the alarm clock ten minutes early on Monday morning. This will redress the balance instantly. If you are groaning inwardly at the idea of a solution to your serial lateness then you are a genuinely rude person who doesn't give a flying fig.

Making Excuses

So what excuses do you use for putting things off? Do you blame other people, or a lack of information or equipment? Do you pretend some jobs are better tackled later in the day? How often do you put things off until it is too late to do them at all? How frequently does this trigger conflict? Do you then resent the 'nagging' that results?

There is a great tendency to take on the easier or more enjoyable jobs first and leave the boring or difficult ones until later. This means that they hover in the air, though, casting a gloom about the day. Procrastination means that ugly pile in your in-tray or those calls from an angry client who you promised to get back to.

I constantly watch staff taking flawed time-management decisions. They are asked to do a very simple and quite urgent task but shelve it, even though they are not particularly busy. Where possible, deal with the small but quite urgent jobs straight away. Then they are off the list, and you feel better.

Dealing With Interruptions

For most of us interruptions occur on a constant basis. To manage your time more effectively, though, you're going to have to start taking charge. Being assertive is one key step. Prioritising is another.

One of the main problems with interruptions is that they are usually man/woman-made, and by rerouting the interrupter we often feel we are being rude and unfriendly.

Open-plan offices mean constant accessibility. If you have your own office, learn to shut the door when you are focused on a priority task. If you have to have an impromptu conversation, try to hold it in the other person's office, or at their desk, so that you decide when to quit. If not, tell people how long you can spare to talk to them.

You can also arrange your desk to make your space less 'visitor-friendly'. If your office looks like a comfortable place for visitors to relax in, then that's usually what they will feel able to do. If your back is to them while you work, or there are no spare chairs in the room, then they will often toddle off more quickly.

Body language is a useful tool for cutting interruptions short. Slapping your hands down on to your thighs is usually effective, with a polite but expectant smile on your face. If all else fails, forget subtlety and look at your watch with a sudden expression of horror.

CHAPTER FOURTEEN

Speed Reading

Quick Tips

◆ Assist your concentration by defining why you are reading the book or document.

◆ Make sure you are comfortable and your book or screen is at the right level.

◆ Take breaks.

◆ Scan through the entire document first, to get familiar with the structure and layout.

◆ As you read more thoroughly, delete bits and highlight bits. Be selective.

◆ Use your finger or pen as a 'speeder'.

◆ Stop reading 'out loud'.

The two skills that made me envy Superman the most were his X-ray vision and his ability to speed-read books. Unfortunately I can't teach you to see through walls, but I can show you how to scan literature more quickly. So here goes.

Stage One

◆ Know *why* you are reading the document. What is your purpose in doing so?

- Are you reading for entertainment or information?

- If you are hunting for information, what is it you need to know?

- What do you already know about the subject?

Then:

- Familiarise yourself with the overall layout or structure of the document. Flip from front to back. Get acquainted with the format.

- Read the summary (the blurb) of the book.

- Scan the chapter headings and delete any subjects that will not be of use to you.

- Highlight any that will (use a highlighter pen if the document or book belongs to you and is not a precious item or keepsake).

- Go on to read the first paragraph of each chapter. From this more detailed research carry on deleting and highlighting, to narrow your area of focus.

Stage Two

- Focus your mind before more detailed reading.

- Get rid of distractions.

- Read when you are in the right mood, not when you are irritable or upset.

- Read when you are calm. Stress inhibits the power to assimilate information.

- Read with an open mind. If you have assumptions about the subject or author that are wrong you will waste time.

◆ Sit in a 'good' position. Be comfortable but not so relaxed you might nod off.

◆ Use your hands. Remember how you used to run your finger along the line when you read as a child? Use the same technique to give your reading rhythm and pace. It will add speed in the same way that the metronomic foot helps your brain maintain impetus. The finger will *make* your eyes keep up a faster speed. It will also focus you on the right spot on the page. This can be especially useful with 'distracting' documents, like newspapers, where several articles, pictures or headlines will all be competing for your attention at one time. You can use a finger or even a pen to provide this pace and focus. Move it smoothly along the line.

◆ This finger or pen can even help you skip-read. If you find you are coasting through a piece you are familiar with, you can take the finger down the middle of the page or along the margin, instead of working each line. If you find there are patches you don't need, you can pull the finger more quickly down the middle until you find a new piece you need to digest.

◆ Use active reading techniques as you go. Keep Post-its handy to mark your page and highlighter pens to mark your document. Make notes in the margin, if necessary.

◆ If you want to absorb and memorise as you read, write key points down on a separate sheet of paper. These will act as a memory-jogger and aid assimilation as you go.

◆ Learn to read with your subconscious mind. This can take in text at a much faster rate than your vocal mind. You should be taking the words in without hearing them or mentally repeating them as they are digested. One sign of over-digesting is if you are reading out loud, i.e. repeating the words under your breath. This means you are too laboured in your working style. Relax. Your mind can absorb what is written on the page without 'hearing' each word as well.

◆ If you 'listen' to each word as you read, you are sticking to old reading techniques taught in primary school. This was where you were taught to hear each letter as a sound. If you work like this you will only ever read at the same speed you speak: approx 180 words per minute. This will be a non-variable. You will never master the technique of speed reading. Learn to go from word to thought missing the sound signal in between.

◆ 'Visual' reading takes practice. At first you will find you aren't really understanding what you have read. Keep at it, though. After a while your understanding will increase to the same levels as when you were doing 'vocal' reading.

Stage Three

Remember what you have read. There is no such thing as a bad memory, unless it has been caused by ill-health. Improve your storage and retrieval system by:

◆ Paying full attention while you are reading. Remember, focus and time-lock!

◆ Making yourself interested in the subject matter.

◆ Having a full understanding of your text. If there are words that you are unfamiliar with, take time to look them up.

◆ Use association techniques while you read. When you get to a part you wish to store away, take small pauses to create visual associations in your mind. *See* the stuff you are reading about. Connect it to your own experiences. See how you will be using the knowledge.

◆ Stop yourself drifting. The brain needs very little excuse to go walkabout. Try an experiment to see. Count slowly from one to a hundred. See how many numbers you get to before your brain tires of this activity and starts to drift. Your reading materials *ought* to be more interesting, but even so it is hard to maintain focus. Invent a small punishment or 'check' gesture to bring your focus back every time you feel the drift. This can be a light tap on the hand or arm, or a flick on the side of the face. Or you could just repeat the command 'focus' to bring your attention back into line.

Stage Four

Look after your eyes. Eye strain will make you revert to bad reading habits:

◆ Read by good light. This should be soft but illuminate the book evenly.

◆ Keep moving your eyes to focus middle distance at regular intervals.

◆ Develop your skills of reading by peripheral vision. Take your eye to the middle word on each line and try to read the entire line without moving your focus.

◆ If you are reading off your screen, make sure the contrast is good.

◆ Ensure the screen is at a comfortable height and angle.

◆ Ensure there is no outside light reflecting off the screen into your eyes.

◆ Stretch your body and give your eyes a little workout by varying focus and rolling them around about every twenty minutes.

PART THREE

Life Skills

CHAPTER FIFTEEN

Getting a Life

'Time, not money, is for many the barrier to a richer life.'

RESEARCH DIRECTOR, DR MICHAEL WHITE

Your time outside work may be precious to you, or it may not. You may live to work or work to live – or perhaps you have an ideal of a harmonious balance between the two.

Work–Life Balance

I have touched on the work–life balance earlier in this book, but it needs some more focused attention here. It has been the hottest initiative to hit business in a long time. It emerged as a counter-point to the 1990s cult of 'Burn 'em out early', where downsizing was king and employees were expected to over-extend in terms of hours worked and effort paid in an attempt to make up the staff ration deficits. It is home working and controlling your hours. It should mean investing in a life outside the workplace, leaving earlier and catching sight of your family.

But I think the idea is, in practice, deeply flawed.

It should work. If you were the nation's doctor you would have looked at that stressed-out, overworked workforce toiling their long hours and you would have said: install a policy of work–life balance, too. But, for the idea to succeed, like many business ideas, you would have had to hang around for long enough to make sure people were doing it *properly*.

Work–life balance has failed in many companies because of its ambiguity. It has become yet another 'concept' that employees adopted in word, but rarely in deed. In some firms it has acquired the 'so-called' tag, as in 'so-called open-door policy' and 'so-called mission statement', as in the company talks about it a lot but does nothing in reality. In others it has become a new demand to be placed upon the employees themselves, rather than the company that employs them, like stress management and (even) time management.

Instead of healing at source and freeing employees to spend time at home, some companies have retained their usual demands while expecting employees to provide additional proof of their holistic ability, as in 'I work nine hours a day but I also work out/play golf/raise ten kids/run marathons/climb mountains', etc.

You Decide for *You*

The main flaw of the phrase work–life balance is that it appears to presuppose distinctions between the two. Yet, for most people, work is a facet of life. Dividing the two into separate camps, even just perceptually, can cause problems. It should be up to you to balance your time and your activities as fairly as possible but it doesn't always help to see work and life as different things. Many people allow their jobs to be the most important thing in their life. For others it might be children, or relaxation or a leisure interest.

Some people arrange their working lives to suit different phases. They may spend some years committing totally to their job, making long hours and semi-permanent involvement the norm. Then they may move on to a less work-committed phase where they lie fallow, workwise, for a while.

Some people prefer their job to friendships and leisure

pursuits. Some go to work to escape from home life. Not everyone is living in an idyllic relationship and home circumstances. When managers sit on the beach taking calls from the office it may be that they are heartily appalled at the prospect of making sand castles and riding the waves on floaty bananas.

Only you can decide your own long- and short-term plans and objectives. Where a rethink becomes crucial is when you feel trapped in a spiral of overwork that is making it impossible to see enough of your family and friends, and when seeing more of your family and friends is, for you, a prime life objective.

If your goal in business time management was to quit work earlier and spend more time at home then you may not quite see the value of social time management. Our every waking hour, though, is spent doing things that we *want* to do, things that we *have* to do, or things that we feel we *ought* to be doing. If you spend too much of your home time on the *haves* and *oughts*, then maybe you need to engineer more free time for the *wants*.

Haves and Oughts

We all have to do the *haves* and *oughts*, but the objective is to spend less time doing them. This may require some massive change in both lifestyle and thinking, but I can promise you it is worth it.

Working the Home

Your ideas of how a house should be run will result directly from your experiences in childhood. The standards you live at now will have been affected by this, plus a degree of input from whomever else you currently live with. Your own childhood home will have become your role model in either a positive or negative way. The things our parents do are either copied by us or so reviled by us that we become a complete opposite. So if your parents were obsessively neat you may be a slob, or vice versa.

Rearranging your workplace to become more time-efficient is easier than rearranging your home. At work you started with a clean sheet, with very little in the way of role models. Your teaching for home behaviour started early. Too early, possibly, to make total change feasible. You may have to do battle with behaviours and assumptions you learnt before the age of seven.

Another problem is getting communal buy-in from whoever you share your home with. They may not want to change. If you've been doing the lion's share of the housework, for instance, and are just discovering the fairness of delegation, they most likely won't want to change. Or they may merely baulk at an alteration of timings and rituals. Even a small tweak can have a ripple effect.

I was brought up in the era of 'women do the housework'. Men went to work and women cleaned and had kids. Sometimes there was a variation where women *also* went to work, but then they also cleaned and they also had kids, too. I now know better. I know what is fair. But I still feel guilty when I see a bloke dusting or cooking his own dinner. I know it's right but it goes against my cultural upbringing. I hope you accept it as a historical norm.

But the lure is still there. If a man wants to look completely and utterly adorable to other women, all he needs to do is borrow a well-scrubbed small child and wheel it in an empty trolley round Tesco's. Most women still feel that primeval pull to join in and help and take over. Whereas, as far as I know, a lone woman with child and trolley in Tesco's has about as much chance of pulling a bloke as Bernard Manning in drag.

Guilt

A major feature of home time management is guilt. You may be motivated by guilt, if, for instance, your job means you spend too little time watching the kids grow up. Or you may find guilt is a by-product of home time management, if, for instance, you decide to stop home baking and dish up shop-bought instead. Or you take shortcuts with the cleaning. Or you start delegating chores you could do to outside agencies. But just think of all that time freed up to either laze about or do a hobby. Imagine the joy of swanning off on holiday and coming back to find your home has been repainted, rather than burgled.

You have four core options when it comes to most household tasks:

1. Do it yourself.

2. Delegate internally.

3. Delegate externally.

4. Let it rot.

CHAPTER SIXTEEN

Delegating in the Home

Cleaning is the great Time Bandit, but each of the delegation options has a certain degree of success attached. So, to look at the options:

1 DIY

Yes, it can be quicker to do it yourself, after all you could have that hoover round the carpet in half the time it takes to persuade someone else to do it or find a cleaner who has got references from the royal family downward. But think about your long-term time management. Doing it means *always* doing it. Delegation means a degree of time-investment but a long-term massive saving.

2 Internal Delegation

This means sharing chores between family or flatmates. This will probably mean some serious negotiations. But what you are heading towards is something that is not only time saving for you but also *fair*.

Remember *karoshi*? Don't work yourself to death.

Delegation

This is as serious a concept in the home as it is at work. Avoid doing things that you can get someone else to do for you, unless you love doing them. Internal delegation can either come free, as in: relatives or friends, or it can come cheap, as in kids who want paying.

Delegating tasks to your family requires clever dialogue. The first thing you need to realise is that this is not delegation in the truest sense. These tasks do not *belong* to you, and, by doing them, your family are not doing you a *favour*. Start with that approach and you are a sucker.

Motivation

Give reasons for tasks. If there aren't any, don't do them. No sane person should be forced to change a broderie anglaise toilet-roll holder because the job clearly doesn't make sense. Washing clothes makes sense. Taking the rubbish out makes sense. The roll holder is just your little foible. Expect a fight if you try to enforce it as a task.

Expect other members of your family to have differing ideas as to what constitutes 'tidy'. It's fair to negotiate this one. You may think tidy means the shagpile has all been combed in one direction. Someone else may see 'tidy' as meaning you can still see sections of the floor beneath all the piled junk. There is no real right or wrong here, just taste. Be assertive in your discussions and avoid the use of phrases like: 'You've got to' and 'or else'.

How to persuade someone to tidy his/her own room

♦ If there are bigger issues at stake, such as the last throes of the 'Do as I tell you' parent–child struggle, then skip the issue with the room and discuss the bigger picture. Cut to the quick.

♦ Never use threats as in 'If you don't tidy your room I will throw everything out on to the street.' Teenagers hold the trump cards. They can leave home and make you think they're living in cardboard boxes.

♦ Never tidy the room yourself.

- Never push too hard. Push creates resistance.

- Look at the situation in transactional analysis terms. Your teenager has allowed his/her room to become scruffy by behaving in his/her 'free child' state. The dirt is a sign of spontaneity and creativity. It's not supposed to be offensive, it's just there. It occurred, it wasn't made.

When you called the first cry to battle with the phrase 'You've *got* to tidy your room' you created an *order*. This meant you were acting in Critical Parent mode, as in 'I'm right, you're wrong.' This in turn jettisoned your poor Free Child into the state of Rebellious Child. He/she had little room to manoeuvre. The only alternative would have been to clean the room, in which case he/she would have been moving to Compliant Child, i.e. passive, which would mean he/she would grow up to be a right wuss.

Once your teenager moves to Rebellious Child the battle becomes more important than the issue. Backing down is impossible. It can be the same struggle with clothing or eating. Push results in resist. Neither side backs down and deadlock is achieved. Deadlock is time-consuming. Try moving to another ego state to break the deadlock. Here are some alternatives:

Adult: sit down and have a rational discussion about the problem and relevant issues.

Nurturing parent: tell them you're worried about their health living in a room like that and offer to redecorate it in a style that they will love more.

3 External Delegation

This means:

- Hiring full-time staff.

- Booking a cleaner direct, or

- Getting cleaners from an agency.

Full-time staff is my ultimate dream, but then I was reared on TV programmes like *Upstairs, Downstairs*. I would love my home to run like clockwork, even when I'm not there but especially when I am.

Booking a freelance cleaner will involve a lot of asking around. This is OK, but don't expect too much of references from friends. The people they swear are absolute angels who work for next to nothing will often morph into the cleaner from hell the minute he or she hits your homestead.

I have never hired a cleaner but evidently you end up chatting to them and stopping them working. There can also be a tendency to clean before they arrive, in case your dirtiness appals them. I can understand this but cleaning for the cleaner is obviously a wasteful use of time.

Getting a cleaner from an agency may be more expensive than booking direct, but it should mean you are covered if one cleaner is off sick. You only have the agency to deal with, and if you're not happy with some aspect of the work, the more passive employer might find it easier giving feedback to an agency than face to face with the person involved.

CHAPTER SEVENTEEN

Home Improvements

There is a kind of sod's law about tidiness and cleaning. You can scrub, dust and polish all your life in case of unexpected guests. Only they never turn up when the place is looking neat. Unexpected guests only arrive the minute the cat has been sick on the carpet.

You can spend your entire time indoors dressed in co-ordinating kaftans *à la* Margo Leadbetter, but unexpected guests only arrive when you drag on those old Lycra leggings from the charity bag because you're only cleaning out the drains.

House-proud

Only be house-proud if you enjoy it or if you can't afford to get someone else to do it. If you are busy or under-financed then pick a lifestyle that suits your circumstances.

The Big Tidy is more creative than daily dusting. De-junk your house. Blitz the entire place. Dedicate a weekend to it. If you don't have the time, do it instead of Easter or Christmas. You will love the after-effect. And so will your house. Set about the place with plastic bin-bags. If the junk is extreme hire a skip.

Go through cupboards and be brutal. Throw things out or sell them at a boot fair.

'I want to keep it because it may become a collector's item'

The phrase 'collector's item' is usually only applied to real junk. As you get older you'll always find there were toys and ornaments that got thrown out that appear later on *The Antiques Roadshow*. But think of the complete and utter chaos of the junk you'd have to live in to hedge all your bets. If in two minds, take it to the charity shop or sell it yourself.

If people die and you inherit more junk, just keep one item as a memento and throw the rest out. Parents should make this proviso in their will because to do otherwise is cruel.

Clutter creates chaos in the mind as well as the house. If you prefer an intentionally busy look, like Victorian style, then fine. It's the unintentional clutter I'm asking you to junk.

Home Filing

This sounds sad, because filing should be a workplace duty, but you know that it works. Buy a large box file and keep household documents in different compartments. Or keep a desk for the household documents. (Photocopy any really valuable ones just in case.) This is hard to do but easy to maintain and wonderful to enjoy the effects of. The three best home timekeeping habits I have learnt are:

1. File documents.

2. Stop writing phone numbers and messages on to scraps of paper.

3. Don't have kids.

Keeping Control of Your Chores – Future Planning

Dusting (steps to minimise)

Buy an old property and old furniture. They're supposed to look dingy. Use Miss Haversham in *Great Expectations* as a role model. Trendy, minimalist flats and houses may appear OK as they have less things in them to dust, but they sure do show up dirt. Chrome, glass, light-coloured carpets and tiled surfaces all look great when you're apartment-viewing but less good a couple of weeks later when things have been splashed, dripped on and scratched. If you choose modern minimalist, expect to spend extra hours cleaning. Even cleaners baulk at working in a loft conversion. So pick a form of middle-minimalist if you want an easier time of it. Or do as I suggest and pick old.

Antiques

◆ Buying from auctions save time. The bidding is quick and so are the delivery times, because they don't have long-term storage space. You could fill your house in one evening, if you wanted. All you need to do is view beforehand, arriving with a pencil and a measuring tape. If you're looking for colour matches then take swatches with you, too. You don't even need to attend the auction, you can bid by phone or leave a written bid. Written bids are good because you can't exceed your ideal price.

◆ When you are measuring up, though, measure corridor and door widths, too. I once bought something that wouldn't go through the front door.

◆ Most local auction houses have a mixture of antiques, junk and newer furniture. You don't always have to spend a fortune on a Ming vase, there are good bargains there, too.

Old stuff makes for great, time-efficient, interior design. You're not worried about superficial damage because most of it has been done before you bought it. If you're buying repro you'll probably find some poor sod has spent ages making it look distressed, anyway.

Trendy old stuff is already dirty, too. Some of it is threadbare and ragged. This gives the 'museum' look to your property. Antique upholstery, in particular, can be particularly distressed.

Bare, varnished floorboards are the best time-saving option in any house. They need dusting, rather than hoovering, but even that can be done relatively speedily: tie two dusters to your feet and just swan around the floor for a bit.

Carpets

If you must have these then you're going to have to head for the vacuum cleaner. Infrequent hoovering means buying a carpet in a colour that doesn't show marks. The best is probably that kind of motley-oatmeal stuff that blends into anything.

Carpet tiles

I once saw a woman with a really good time-saving wheeze. She'd put carpet tiles over her entire floor. I discovered how they worked when her dog was sick, though. She whipped the offending tile up, dangled it under the tap, shook it to dry and popped it back in place again. This woman had three cats, two dogs and two small children, so there was quite a lot of puking in her house. So she had eschewed aesthetics and found something that saved her heaps of time. Sluttish it may have looked, but sometimes sluttishness is time-effective.

Work Surfaces

A lot of aesthetically pleasing work surfaces are horrendous to clean. I know I suggested old stuff in your house but that doesn't apply to the kitchen. Victorian women may have scrubbed until their bustles wiggled, but sod that for a game of soldiers. Wiping should be the most cleaning you do in your kitchen. I inherited a slate work surface in my current house and it is wonderful. It doesn't show stains and it wipes down a treat. What I also inherited, though, were 'country-kitchen' style wooden unit doors with beading. Forget beading. Nooks collect dirt, and beading is like one big nook. Kitchen dirt is greasy, too. Cleaning the beading involves heavy-duty scrubbing. Don't go there. Buy flush surfaces instead.

Quick Cleaning

◆ Clean chrome taps with white vinegar on a cloth.

◆ Clean the hard gunk off the shower head by tying a plastic bag filled with white vinegar round the head and leaving it to marinate overnight. Give it a scrub the next day.

◆ Throw a couple of fizzy false-teeth tablets into the loo overnight. It will be gleaming by morning.

◆ To stop your microwave getting that stale smell, put a bowl of water into it with a tablespoon of lemon juice and cook on high for 30 seconds.

◆ To wash a decanter, fill it with cold water then turn it upside down and run cold water from the tap full force on the base.

◆ Soak burnt pans in cold tea.

◆ When something in the oven spills and starts smoking, chuck salt over the spill.

◆ Get those white, coffee-mug ring marks out of wood by rubbing mayonnaise in and leaving it overnight.

◆ Get stains out of tea towels by laying them out on the lawn overnight.

◆ Use shaving cream to get spot stains off the carpet.

◆ Get pet hairs off carpets and settees by rubbing them down with rubber gloves on your hands.

◆ Put bay leaves in cupboards to keep cockroaches out.

Display Items

Avoid these like the plague in your kitchen. Knives, mug trees, utensil holders, egg holders, things to hang bananas from – these are objects from hell when it comes to cleaning. What you can dust quickly in the rest of the house has to be scoured regularly in the kitchen. If you keep things in cupboards they keep cleaner longer.

De-junk Your Kitchen

Go through all those cupboards and drawers and throw out anything that you don't use or need. People keep the most horrible things just because they have been given as a gift or are frightened they might 'come in handy' one day.

If you feel guilty about getting rid of gifts, then give them to charity. No giver could ever possibly complain about that.

Why Decant?

This is a strange habit. Worse still, it is time-consuming. The only things worth decanting are perishables, like biscuits or cereals that would go stale or soft otherwise. Even biscuit packets can be made self-seal if you eat the top four in one go and then use tape on the folded package. Most packaging looks OK and is disposable, whereas decanting holders need cleaning.

Gardening

This can be a great hobby, but only for the seriously under-employed. I once went on an 'open day' of local gardens in North London. They were, without exception, breathtakingly beautiful. None were bigger than the average large city garden but all of them were immaculately tended. Their owners showed us visitors around with pride but they all, again without exception, had turned their garden into their life. It was a full-time pursuit.

This is fine if this is the sort of life you want to lead. If not, plump for the smaller, patio-style garden or live in a flat with nothing bigger to tend than a window box. And never fall for some of the more obvious 'easy-tend' wheezes that turn out to be time disasters.

Leaves go of their own accord

I spent my first year with a garden with trees watching in horror as the leaves dropped in autumn. I decided a policy of 'clear up as they drop' would save time. I was out there every day raking and shoving the leaves into bin-bags, and then bribing the bin-men to take the bin-bags away. The next year I was writing a novel and so didn't have time to go clearing up leaves. And guess what? They went. Leaves vanish of their own accord. I don't know where to. A bit of a breeze and they're off.

Just a few tips for wannabe gardeners whose ambition is larger than their experience:

◆ Put shorter plants at the front and taller at the back.

◆ Only buy plants with the words 'hardy' on the label.

◆ Scour your local area, studying other gardens, looking for plants that seem to like the soil and conditions and buy those.

◆ Never work from seed or cuttings.

◆ Plant a garden that will look good overgrown.

◆ Plant lots of ivy.

◆ Use a mix of yoghurt and fertiliser to get stone ornaments to moss-up quickly.

CHAPTER EIGHTEEN

Fast-track Hosting for Dinner Parties

The days of the marathon dinner party seem to be over, thank God. They were a staple part of every stress martyr's repertoire, when you booked a dinner party for forty in the middle of some sort of workplace crisis and then spent hours, if not days, peeling, chopping, marinating, simmering and stuffing. If you were truly up for it you would embroider the tablecloth, hand-etch the glassware and crotchet the doilies yourself, too.

You *definitely* made the after-dinner chocolates yourself, and they always looked like cat's poo. One hostess I know even made water biscuits by hand. If you could boast that you grew or hand-reared the produce as well you gained several extra points on the martyr-ometer. Then you would do one of three things during dinner:

1. Fall asleep at the table.

2. Throw hysterics in the kitchen.

3. Get badly pissed and do both.

Takeaway

Forget the set-piece dinner parties. Invite friends round and get out the takeaway menu. Working people love this because they can reciprocate without tears. The real horror of set-piece dinner parties is to sit eating someone else's marinated goats' cheese in filo with bilberry jus and hand-carved French beans that have been plaited into baskets, and know it is your turn next time.

If you want to look as though you're suffering a bit, decorate the table with Indian fabrics, buy a Ravi Shankar CD, and string fairy lights out in the garden.

Or you can go down the old M & S route, spearing cartons with forks and letting the microwave ping away happily.

One tip – *be honest*. To be stylish you do need to be honest. If you serve takeaway, tell your guests. Wondering who the late arrival is when the delivery boy rings and then shouting out that it was the door-to-door cleaner salesman while you decant balti from foil containers into antique china is far too blatantly dishonest, as is pretending the M & S was home-cooked. (They'll only spot the cartons in the swing-bin and then ask questions about the recipe, just to wind you up.)

Caterers

Or you could get your dinner party catered, if you can stand the expense and potential disruption. Many restaurants offer this service now, so it's worth checking out costs. I would worry about having other people in my kitchen and the cleaning-fest that would have to occur before the caterers arrive but you might be more readily prepared.

If you can afford caterers who serve and clear away – great. That way you get hosted like everyone else and just sit back and get drunk without worrying about the cat getting to the salmon mousse.

Dinner Parties at Restaurants

These can be great fun because all you have to do is turn up and pay up. Most places have private rooms and set menus, so these can be less extortionate that you might think. I started using them for family birthdays and became hooked. They're not a cheap option, but neither are home-cooked banquets. Pick a time when the restaurant is usually quiet and negotiate on cost.

Dinner Parties Where You Delegate the Cooking

I haven't quite got into this culture but I know hosts who swear by it. The idea is that everyone brings a course, which shares the hassle and cost of the meal. Be cautious and plan well if you try this. The dangers are:

◆ Guests get competitive and start doing elaborate courses. This can lead to a badly balanced meal, with each course so rich that stomach pumps and enemas are the order of the day.

◆ Someone drops out at the last minute. That someone is usually responsible for some sort of vital ingredient, like the main course, or the booze.

◆ Everyone turns up clutching food encased in multiple bowls. You become responsible for washing up more dishes than normal and then relocating them over the following week.

◆ People turn up with half-prepared dishes that they expect to finish off in your kitchen.

Short-cut Catering

If you are cooking the whole meal, remember these five time-saving tips:

1. Do food that looks good but is easy and quick to prepare. Tart dishes up like they do in restaurants with a dribble of sauce, a few shavings of Parmesan, a quick shake-over of icing sugar, etc.

That way you can use simple, fresh and possibly raw ingredients that look classy and clever.

2. Serve up quick, simple stuff like sausages, cheese and pineapple on sticks, and packet trifle, and claim you are making an ironic statement, like Jeffrey Archer did when he served shepherd's pie with champagne at his parties.

3. Serve strong Martini cocktails before eating.

4. Never tell people what they are eating. When you start identifying dishes by name people's expectations start to rise. Let them work it out for themselves.

5. Don't let guests help with the washing up. It only means you'll have to do it when you visit them.

Cooking and Clearing

Recipe books should come with details of how much mess will be left to clear up once you are finished. Do a quick mental assessment while you read the recipe through. Time spent on the dish itself is only time saved if the clearing away is minimal, too.

CHAPTER NINETEEN

Organising Your Wardrobe

Now, there are not many things I like to organise with military precision in the house, but my wardrobe is one of them. The reason for this is that I am a compulsive shopper and if I fail to tidy and prune at the same rate as I buy I become quickly overrun. I have already had to move house once to cope with my wardrobe. People who ask why a couple with no kids need a six-bedroom house are people who don't know me or my buying habits.

You may have a pint-size wardrobe already, but I expect – like most people's – there is some room for improvement in its over-all layout. Do you need to be told why wardrobe management is such a vital facet of time-management? Well, there are three main benefits to a wardrobe you can whip through speedily:

1. Getting ready for work is much, much faster. Things hang well and are maintained, so that you spend less time ironing or dithering when the outfit you had decided to wear is discovered being used as a dog blanket.

2. A tidy wardrobe means a more stress-free mind. There is something rewarding and virtuous about opening cupboard doors and being master of all you survey. A tidy wardrobe sets you on the path towards a tidier life.

3. Knowing what you already have makes shopping faster.

Organising your wardrobe is a lot like organising your desk. For a start, you will need several large bin-bags and a degree of calm patience. Be prepared to forward invest on this one. Tidying will take a lot of time but save more than that invested over the next few months. A well-organised wardrobe will be low maintenance. Once the initial work is done it will only require some on-the-spot hanging and folding. The sight of all those tidy clothes will be sufficient inspiration for this.

A couple of questions before you start:

1. Do you have enough room for your clothes or do you have to store some? And,

2. Do you have a schizophrenic wardrobe, i.e. does it have to service several different lifestyles?

If you store, then the obvious step is to store according to season. Never store according to 'clothes I like' and 'clothes I'm not sure about' because the latter bunch will rarely get to see the light of day. Clothes are never ever better than you remembered. If you thought that suit was trash then it will only improve in your memory. Digging around for it some three years later will only mean you waste time searching and then cleaning and ironing, only to discover as you try it on again that it was every bit as hideous as it was originally.

Never keep clothes in the hope that they will come back into fashion again. *Looks* come back into fashion but clothing doesn't. The only sort that does is real retro, i.e. stuff you are too young to have worn the first time around.

Packing clothes for storage is difficult. I would suggest you fold them around white tissue to prevent creasing, but in reality the creasing is going to happen whatever. Sometimes it's quicker just to bite the bullet and chuck them into the bin-bags.

If your attic is big enough you could store them hanging. Buy a collapsible metal clothes rail and keep them pristine. Never put thin dry-cleaner's plastic bags over them because the plastic draws dirt via static. Cloth bags are better.

The better the hanger the better the life and look of the outfit, whether you are storing or using. The big wooden ones are best, but failing that buy the wide, black plastic ones. Store skirts and trousers on the expandable hangers that hang from the waist. Never fold them over a middle bar or hang them from the tabs as they will always need ironing before you wear them.

Mothballs are vital when you are storing. Never buy the sort that reek of camphor. Modern plastic ones are virtually odour-free.

Shoes are probably best stored in shoeboxes. Push tissue into the toes first.

Use shoeboxes for storing packets of tights, too. You can file them upright, with one box for flesh tights and another for colours. Buy in bulk when you shop.

Your Current Wardrobe

This may need subdividing. I have one rail for formal business-wear and one for casual. Mixing the two is a big mistake in time terms. Your casual gear can be thrown together at random but your business stuff needs to be low maintenance and easy mix and match.

If your company does dress-down Fridays then you may need to sub-subdivide, with two work wardrobes. I know the intention is to wear normal causal on dress-down days but in reality this never works. What a company sees as 'casual' is rarely the same sort of look that sane people would wear on their days off. You may need to reserve a separate section of your clothes rail for your dress-down range.

Organise your work wardrobe according to colour, starting with the lightest tones at the front and the darkest at the back. If you want the best time-productive and low-maintenance work wardrobe you should chose one base colour, usually a non-fashion-dependent shade, like black or navy, and buy all your trousers, skirts and jackets either in that colour or in shades that tone with it. Having one base colour for your working wardrobe means faster and easier daily mix and match.

Your base colour for the summer should also be fairly neutral. Pick a shade that suits your skin tone and one that you are unlikely to grow too tired of.

Less is more for your business wardrobe. Some of the best-dressed city people rotate their way through four to five suits and a handful of shirts or tops. You don't need to make huge statements to look stylish at work. Do it with the cut and fit of the suit, or via clever accessories.

◆ Ties should be hung or rolled and stored in a shallow drawer. Get them dry-cleaned regularly.

◆ Keep your work shoes stored in racks at the bottom of the wardrobe. Polish your shoes when you take them off, rather than when you put them on as you may not have time in the morning.

◆ Jumpers should be folded or hung over padded hangers.

◆ Dry-clean your suits regularly. Never trouser-press a pair of trousers that need cleaning as it will 'cook' the dirt into the fabric.

◆ Investigate the possibility of an office dry-clean delivery service. This means the dry-cleaners come to you, rather than the other way around.

◆ Always empty pockets when you take clothes off at night.

◆ Hang the garment to air before replacing it in the wardrobe.

◆ Dry-cleaners often have a shirt laundry service. Check out prices.

◆ When you buy a business suit, buy an extra pair of trousers as these often age faster than the jacket.

◆ Never hang your jacket over the back of your chair at work as it ruins the shape.

◆ Always carry a sewing kit for on-the-spot repairs, plus a dry-clean spot remover.

- ◆ Keep two smallish drawers, one for business socks or tights that are all identical and one for business underwear in flesh colour.

- ◆ Carry spare tights or socks.

- ◆ Keep at least one spare tie in your drawer at work.

Packing for Business Travel

- ◆ Place all your heavy items, like toiletries, in first. Put them on top and they'll crease your clothes.

- ◆ Then fill gaps with your underwear, or roll these between folds to help minimise creasing.

- ◆ Pack a layer of shirts and tops and then finish with suits.

- ◆ Or use a lightweight hanging suit bag.

- ◆ Buy crease-free garments for travel. They may not look as good as pure fibres but you can jettison style for smartness.

- ◆ Keep a space for something cosy to wear lounging in your bedroom, like a lightweight robe. This will help you to relax and unwind.

- ◆ If you find you've packed too much, lay everything out on the bed and then halve it.

- ◆ Buy at least one pair of shoes that will go with everything.

Homestyle

Your out-of-work clothes will tend to be much more representative of your individuality and it is here that you can afford to go a bit wild. Even so there is scope for some time management.

Work/evening wear has always been a fascinating concept. Magazines are full of natty suits that turn into swish cocktail outfits at the drop of a bra strap. The usual suspect is the 'Little

Black Dress'. These, of course, stink. I have bought two in my lifetime and have worn neither. The nearest thing I ever did get to a success was a black silk tube that was ruched, like a swimming costume. I wore it off the shoulder and it clung all the way down. Its main use was that it packed to the size of a condom and never needed ironing.

Sarongs are great because they really can be used to good effect. There are the summer cotton ones for beach-to-bar and the chiffon variety with some glittery embroidery that you can use anywhere. You can drape them over a dull work suit or you can tie them over trousers. Take your jacket off when you are going from the office to a date and wrap the sarong over your trousers for a stunning effect.

Men are slightly more stuffed when it comes to day-to-evening wear, but then most business suits are acceptable, if a little traditional, for an evening performance. You could take the tie off but that often looks a bit pretentious if the suit is very formal. Or you could buy a raw silk tie in a non-office colour, like peacock blue or lavender. A contemporary suit would be OK with the business shirt swapped for a T-shirt.

Your Wardrobe Makeover

You are going to de-junk your wardrobe. Take everything out of your wardrobe, throwing it into one of three piles as you do so:

1. Garments that are in good condition and instantly wearable.

2. Garments that need altering, cleaning or repairing, or which are out of season.

3. Garments you don't wear, either because they have performed well and died of old age, or that you have bought and never worn.

Hang the first pile, keeping the business and casual clothes hanging on separate rails. Pack or hang away the out-of-season garments. Take the dry-clean/repair clothes to the cleaners and rehang on proper hangers when they return. Bin the ancient clothes and take the better stuff to the charity shop.

If you find getting rid of good-quality clothes painful, check in the phone book for the nearest second-hand designer shop and take them there. These shops usually take good things and sell them for a commission. This should clear your conscience and help you be more brutal in the clothes you decide to discard.

Never keep a virtual-reality wardrobe, i.e. a rail of clothes that you wish fitted, but which are too small. These never act as an initiative for a diet, they just act as a silent reprimand that is more than enough to send you running to the biscuit tin. All the clothes hanging on your rail should fit.

When your rail is organised, make a shopping list of anything you need to make your wardrobe perfect. Write a full description of what you are looking for, including colour. Shopping can be a confusing experience and it helps to take a specific wish list with you. A swatch of fabric can help with the matching. Snip a small piece from the inside edge of a seam.

CHAPTER TWENTY

Shopping

I love shopping and it would be on my list of 'things I want my working time freed up to do'. But even *I* don't like *all* shopping. I love clothes shops and hate supermarkets, DIY stores and soft furnishing departments. I also hate any shop that gives poor customer service.

Most people I meet hate all shopping, especially for clothes. If this is you it makes you an alien to me, but I do shop for clothes quickly, so am well placed to provide tips. Here are some of the best:

1. Shop early. Clothes shops don't usually turn into a scrum, except during the sales, but queues for tills and changing rooms do build up.

2. Shop during the week, if possible. Weekends will always be busy, although even a Saturday is bearable if you start early.

3. Wear clothes that are easy to take off. Which means no layering and no lace-up shoes.

4. Avoid too much rooting. Work on the 'at a glance' principle. If the fabrics, styles and colours don't appeal to you the minute you walk in then walk straight out again.

5. Ditto when you try on. All the posing in the world won't make a bad fit look better.

6. Recognise highest and lowest prices that you are prepared to pay and shop accordingly.

7. If you are shopping for clothes don't buy anything else at the

same time. Travel light. Even shoes should be bought on a separate day.

8. If you are a terminally bad clothes shopper, remember most large stores provide a personal shopper service, often for free. You tell the shopper your requirements and they pull out anything they think will suit you. Phone ahead to book an appointment.

9. Try to shop alone.

10. Shopping in malls may sound like a good idea but it rarely is. Most of them are soul-destroying and far too uniform in what they have to offer.

11. Shopping in designer retail parks is another matter. Find one that sells real designer wear, not just trainers and sportswear. If you find a good one and you're not a happy clothes shopper, make a biannual pilgrimage to one of these and buy your entire wardrobe in one go.

12. You will often be asked at the till whether you would like to become an account customer. If you want to save money and are not the sort who gets easily seduced into debt then go ahead, but only if you have an hour or so to kill. They will take details and you will have to fill in forms. Save time by saying no. All credit cards come with liability along with the ease of purchase.

13. Get your own chauffeur. Most shopping spots mean difficult parking and you don't want to leave your car, or drag around with your partner. Negotiate with them. Offer a day of freedom in return for a lift back home.

Catalogues

This used to be the worst way to shop and I should know, because I have worked on some of the photo shoots. Clothing used to be made as cheaply as possible and then photographed to look as good as possible. Garments were pinned, tweaked and even stuffed with tissue in an attempt to make them look classy. What arrived in the package was ultimately disappointing, but most people thought it was their own fault for being a funny shape and kept it anyway.

Things have improved now – a bit. Shops like Next offer the same quality merchandise to buy by mail. It arrives speedily and you get to try it on in your home, rather than in a smelly changing room. If you hate visiting the shops or lack time to do so, then catalogues are probably the thing for you.

Shopping On-line

According to HSBC, one in three of us in the UK spend 12 per cent of our income via the telephone or the Internet. Many more of us will soon be shopping via our mobile phones, thanks to WAP. This is the technology that connects us to the Internet via our mobiles. Expect to be booking train tickets, concert seats, flowers and choccies, i.e. all the stuff you buy on-line now, from the comfort of your mobile phone.

On-line shopping sounds like the answer to a maiden's prayer for the time-troubled. I'm not sure it's quite there yet, though. Seeing a garment on screen is not the same as seeing it in the flesh. You need to learn to browse. A quarter of Internet users are already at it and 94 per cent of them said they would be at it on a regular basis in future. The rest of us are probably windy about security and/or confused by the 'how? where? and why?' factor.

How?

You log on to a website and from then on it's pretty much virtual shopping all the way. You usually use a 'shopping cart' which you can fill without commitment until you get to the 'checkout'.

Then you get to revisit your purchases, making changes at random, and then you get asked for your e-mail address and details for payment and delivery. Look for the padlock on screen as a sign of a secure connection between you and the site you are using. This means your details are safe. Usually you can change your mind about a purchase right up until you click on the 'place your order' button. If you're still nervous, some websites allow you to purchase via a phone call. If you find it more convenient, some websites will deliver to your workplace, rather than your home.

◆ When you compare prices with the high street, remember to add on any delivery charge.

◆ Speed of purchase might be offset by delivery deadlines.

◆ Keep your credit card handy when you order.

◆ Check your credit card statements for errors in purchases.

◆ Try to stick to reputable companies.

◆ Keep a record of what you have ordered. Do this by printing the web page.

Where?

Easy – loads of shopping websites, growing on a virtually daily basis.

Why?

◆ Bargains – some products, like books and CDs, are cut price.

◆ Easier – if you hate trawling round malls.

◆ Convenient – you can shop 24 hours.

◆ Faster – if they deliver quickly. At any rate the time spent will be considerably less than if you made the journey to the shop.

Food

Supermarket on-line shopping does interest me as a time-saver, because we probably all spend too long waiting in the trolley queue. There is very little to recommend a trip to the supermarket if you are shopping for bog-standard basics, especially the serial order, like baked beans. Again, I feel this method of shopping will improve with time. Most companies offer a limited list of words, prices and weights at present. I come from the 'see it and grab it' generation. I have no idea what food should weigh. A yoghurt could be 20g, 200g or even 2,000g for all I know. I just know what an individual carton looks like. I felt dyslexic when I stared at the screen. I hadn't realised how much food shopping is done by visual selection. But the food does get delivered, which is marvellous because time spent in hospital having hernias treated is time wasted.

Scroll through the options and get used to shopping for food on-line. If you want to hand-select then pop in for the impulse stuff when you have time.

Making a shopping list is hugely boring but time-fruitful. Make one that is reuseable, rather than rewriting it every week. You probably buy the same stuff anyway. If you laminate the list you can add extra items in felt tip. Keep a chalkboard on the wall of your kitchen. As you run out of things write them up there as a reminder for your weekly shop.

Don't count people when you're looking for the quickest queue, count items in the baskets.

Find a smaller corner shop that you can use for additional buys or forgotten items. Market stalls are great for a speedy transaction because everyone pays cash and they work quickly. Never use one that gets your fruit or veg from the back of the stall, though, especially if it's kept out of sight, as it will probably be rotten.

Buying organic is very worthy. There will be at least a couple of local companies who deliver organic produce. It's quicker than queuing at the farmer's market.

I'm all for convenience foods, anyway. The day M & S brought out ready-peeled potatoes I fell to my knees and blessed their little cotton socks. Ready-peeled does not mean 'bought by sluts'. I just think life really is too short to peel potatoes, that's all. If I buy fresh I cook them in their skins (and yes – I do wash the dirt off first).

Beauty/Grooming

◆ Use long-lasting cosmetic products. Anything too greasy or glossy will tend to be high maintenance. Several make-up brands, like Revlon and Almay, make long-lasting, smudge-free lipsticks and bases.

◆ Clarins make a wonderful stick make-up that blends easily and stays put, without looking or feeling heavy (Clarins Teint Prodige Stick).

◆ Keep one bag or box with no more than one range of cosmetics in it. If your box is too cluttered with alternatives you will take longer in the morning.

◆ Set your make-up with loose powder.

◆ If you want to look fully made-up but only have time to use one or two products, choose lipstick and mascara.

◆ Never have your hair streaked or highlighted – you will die of old age getting it redone each month. Have a rinse or tint put on instead. It may not look as expensive but your hair will have its own natural highlights and you'll save at least one and a half hours every month.

◆ Get a hairstyle that is low maintenance. If you can't just swish your fingers or a brush through it in the morning you don't want it. If it's long just tie it back or plait it for work.

◆ If you have long hair that needs washing but don't have the time, just wash and dry the fringe.

- Shave your legs – it's quicker than other methods.

- Buy quick-dry nail varnish. Most new brands take three to five minutes. Ordinary takes hours.

- Dip your nails into cold water to make the varnish dry quicker.

- Use non-crumbly eyeshadows. Soft powders look great but drop down on to your cheeks as you apply them. Mopping up takes minutes.

- Buy dry shampoo for emergencies.

- Never try to dry hair straight from the shower. It will be too wet for you hairdryer. Allow it to dry naturally for at least fifteen minutes. Eat your breakfast or do your make-up while you're waiting.

- For a quick dandruff shampoo, crush an aspirin into your normal shampoo.

- If your skin gets shiny use a matte skin blotter, either under foundation or instead of it.

- Use two teaspoons from the fridge to calm down puffy eyes.

- If you like using make-up, buy professional palettes. That way you can mix and match colours without having to keep opening tubes and sticks.

- Never get so stuck for time that you do any of your grooming in public. It looks disgusting. Get in a loo somewhere.

- Buy deodorant wipes and keep them at work. In an emergency they will freshen you up for a straight-from-work date. They clean a bit as they deodorise, too. Spraying deodorant over sweat is disgusting.

On-line Banking

Hurrah! No more queues! Cutting bank-queue time out of your life alone must give you back a few days overall in the final tally. Other advantages include:

◆ More control over your finances.

◆ Statements and other details when you want them, rather than at the end of the month.

◆ Getting details from your WAP phone as well.

◆ Competitive interest rates.

How?

Either link up with your current bank or find a new Internet account, in which case you will have to supply proof of identity etc. Then you visit the site whenever by providing security details and set about viewing transactions, switching between accounts, setting up direct debits, etc. If you're making a withdrawal or deposit you do so the normal way, via the bank branch.

CHAPTER TWENTY-ONE

Travel

The most popular purchase on the Internet in the UK is holidays. Around 500,000 people bought holidays in the run-up to Christmas 2000 alone.

Avoiding Jet Lag

Jet lag affects your sleep patterns, body temperature, pulse rate, decision-making and reaction time. Always take precautions to minimise the effects.

◆ Travel with a clear, moisturising face mask that you can apply mid-flight. The air inside a plane is very drying.

◆ Spritz throughout the flight, spraying your face with mineral water.

◆ Avoid all tight clothing.

◆ Wear two watches, one with arrival time and the other with home time. Focus on the new time during each part of the journey.

◆ Try to time your journey so that you sleep as close to your normal bedtime as possible.

◆ Give yourself a break – never time meetings so that you are working straight after arrival. Try to take it easy for the first 24 hours.

◆ Remember that jet lag is twice as bad after eastbound flights as westbound.

◆ Carry some reviving eye drops or wear a soothing, cooling eye mask as you relax on the plane.

Time-managing Your Holiday Preparations

It's easy to be so stressed out by work that you crash the minute you hit the airport. Immune systems have a peculiar way of working. While you are busy at work you may have felt well, owing to the overflow of adrenaline that was the result of multiple crises and emergencies. You can reach a peak as you try to get all your jobs done or ready for handover for the holiday and then, the minute you sit back on your lilo to relax and enjoy the sun, your immune system takes a break too and you fall ill. Or you find yourself so stressed by the travel arrangements that you end up screaming, arguing and ultimately in hysterics before you have left home.

This is known as Holiday Crash. It's the result of stress burn-out on the build-up to your trip and can be avoided with some pre-planning:

◆ Create two brainstormed lists of everything you need to do before you go off. One should be your business list and the other household chores, like cancelling the papers. The original lists can be chaotic, but then tidy them into calendar order and see which jobs can be delegated.

◆ Don't use your holiday as too great a full-stop at work. You don't have to tie up every end just because you're off for two weeks. If anything can wait happily until your return, let it. Just make sure colleagues are aware of the key issues and what action you expect them to take while you are away.

◆ Be careful about leaving contact numbers. If you own the company or work at top-level management you might need or even want to. But even then be very specific about what should be classified a sufficient emergency. Your perception may not be the same as your staff's. If you are anywhere further down the scale I would suggest you become unobtainable. They can manage. If you leave a number you are either trying to prove to yourself that you are indispensable or you are being way too passive.

♦ Work your way through the lists with achievable deadlines. Put similar jobs into clusters, like cancelling milk and newspapers. Be sure to tick things off as you do them. You don't want to be sitting on the plane staring at an unticked item and wondering whether you took the dog to the kennels or not.

♦ Pack and whittle at the same time. Travel light. Buy travel-size versions of all your grooming products, even toothpaste. Things like deodorants and shampoos can weigh a bag down.

♦ Pack one bag of all the things that would scupper your holiday if you left them behind, like passports, essential phone numbers, pills, traveller's cheques, etc. Keep them only in the one place until you arrive, then decide where to keep them for maximum safety. Ask your traveller's cheques supplier for suggestions about keeping them safe en route. You may be asked to store them in a separate bag to the one containing your passport etc.

♦ Start your holiday before you go. Frenzied, last-minute starvation diets will leave you feeling stressed and tired, but a fortnight's healthy lifestyle regime will leave you energised. Eat healthily, exercise and drink plenty of water. Cut down on the alcohol, and have some early nights.

♦ Go shopping but don't panic shop. Last-minute buys for the beach rarely get worn. If you have packed too frugally you can always buy some items on holiday. Most beach spots sell better beachwear than the shops at home.

♦ Be brutal with your holiday reading. Tear out and discard chunks as you have read them. Never take an entire guidebook, either. Just tear out the pages that you need and pack them.

♦ Be calm. People 'catch' panic. If your family and business colleagues sense you are panicking about the holiday they may join in and start making extra demands.

♦ Make sure your luggage is instantly identifiable from a distance. Place matching and eye-catching labels on them all for faster exit from the airport.

♦ Check luggage fastens securely. Expect it to get thrown around by baggage handlers and reinforce with straps, if necessary.

♦ Leave some space in your luggage for any gifts you expect to bring back.

Business Travel

♦ Allow time in your business diary to complete urgent tasks and handovers before you leave.

♦ Don't rush the handovers. Incomplete briefing can spell disaster.

♦ But don't fuss, either. This makes colleagues feel you don't trust their abilities. Allow some ground for empowerment to make and take decisions on your behalf.

♦ Check you know how to access voicemail, fax and e-mail while you are on the hoof. Most firms will expect you to be as accessible as you are when you sit at your desk. Keep up-to-date with passwords. Make sure your own voicemail message lets callers know what date you return and what they should do in the interim.

♦ Don't take extra tasks to fill in time while you are travelling.

Working on the hoof is stressful. Use the time to relax and think, instead. You don't want to arrive jet-lagged. Count the hours per day you will have worked if you start logging on or doing paperwork while you are in the air or on the train, too. Is this the sort of day you would want to put in at the office? It's easy to overwork just because your routine has changed.

◆ The same applies for sitting in your hotel. Hotel rooms can be lonely places when you are travelling alone but it would be better to watch dross on the TV than to sit catching up on work until midnight, just because you are bored.

◆ Don't make your schedule too tight. Allow some time for jet lag. Also sew in some time to sightsee. This will create more effective mental acuity when you get down to business. Even a couple of hours are better than nothing.

◆ Look at all the accessory items you need on your desk and take copies for travelling.

◆ Take extra care with your laptop. Do you really need to use it en route? If not, pack it in your case. Thieves wait in hotel receptions to spot guests with laptops checking in. These are the rooms they then tend to target to rob.

◆ If you are giving a PowerPoint presentation on your visit, keep discs safe and have copies in another bag, just in case.

◆ Do your slides need translation for foreign visits? It will be easier if your hosts can read them in their own language. Or you could have three or more language translations on each slide for multicultural presentations.

◆ Check whether you need adaptors for electrical equipment.

◆ Check whether the hotel has a hairdryer. If not, buy a travel variety.

◆ Always take your own travel alarm clock. Hotel facilities can be unreliable.

◆ Check you have booking numbers for the hotels you are visiting, plus the name that the room was booked under. Confusion and delay arises if your room has been booked under your company name, rather than your own. Keeping the booking number provides evidence if your booking is challenged. Some hotels will happily double-book and then claim no knowledge of the original booking.

◆ If your name is difficult to spell or pronounce, keep a business card handy to present at reception to avoid delays when checking in.

◆ Get used to working on the hoof. Don't allow everything to wait until you are back in the office. When you take messages try to deal with them right away. This routine is easy when you get used to it. Too many people have an 'I'm away – it will have to wait' mentality that leaves calls piling up to stress you out when you get back to the office.

◆ If you travel frequently, keep a bag ready packed with duplicates of all your grooming products and fresh underwear, etc.

◆ Pack mix-and-match garments for maximum mileage.

Also check all the following before you go:

◆ Language – do they all speak English or will you need a translator?

◆ Currency – do you need traveller's cheques? The euro is readily available in most of Europe now, making the need for constant – and possibly expensive – currency changing redundant. In the USA dollar cheques are more highly regarded than cash or plastic.

◆ Cash dispensers now tend to be available around the world, and most provide an English translation of the transaction. Visa cardholders can even download information into

PalmPilots that will locate every cash machine for them. Keep the emergency number handy in case of theft or loss.

◆ Take at least a couple of cards with you – some machines have a tendency to chew up foreign cards on nothing more than a whim.

◆ Dress – what is the climate like? Is it changeable?

◆ Business dress – always check the preferred formal/informal style of the business culture of the country you are visiting.

◆ Culture – check all other core cultural differences, especially in etiquette and business etiquette. Never assume the 'rules' will be the same as ours. You may insult people or even break the law unwittingly.

◆ Immunisation – check your inoculations are comprehensive and up to date.

◆ Emergencies – know what you will do if you lose your passport or wallet or need any help while abroad. Keep consulate and traveller's cheques lost/stolen departments' numbers, plus details of how to contact the local police.

CHAPTER TWENTY-TWO

Relationships

All relationships are hugely time-expensive, but most are worth the investment. Loneliness is no guarantee of effective time management. So go for all the babies, boyfriends and small furry animals you want, but first make sure they fit into your overall life plan.

Keeping Pets

Pets are great and I love them. I would like to have a yard full of the things, but I don't have time to spend cleaning, walking, tending and feeding.

Don't think that the smaller the pet, the less the trouble. Tiny pets can take lots of time to care for. Little things in cages are regularly let out of cages for 'a bit of a run'. Only they either don't hear or don't understand the word 'bit' and go off on the mother of all runs. It can take hours to find them and recage them. Even goldfish take some looking after. Pets of any size can get sick, too, and whatever the size of pet the time and money spent is often the same.

Cats are probably the easiest pets to care for because, by and large, they like to amuse themselves. If you get two then they don't get lonely while you are out. But they do deserve a garden and shouldn't be kicked out near a busy road. And they can decimate your three-piece suite.

Dogs are more like babies in time-terms. They need balanced feeding, constant attention and loads of clearing up after.

Cats have to be left behind when you travel but a dog can share your trip and even keep you company.

If time is an issue with you, make sure you never scrimp if you're taking on a pet. All pets take commitment and commitment involves time.

Babies

- *More than half of women with children under five return to work.*

- *Only 5 per cent of employers provide workplace nurseries.*

You're out on your own with children. I see them as the biggest Time Bandit of the lot, but then the rewards obviously outweigh the inconvenience. Having a child means dedicating a whole chunk of your life to another person. Holding a job down too is heroic in my eyes, but then most people do it. There is something very personal about the child time-commitment issues. Some mothers pause between meetings to give birth and are back in the saddle as soon as the nanny arrives. Others retire from the workplace at the mere thought of conception. I won't even begin to give you advice because it is your choice.

A colleague of mine has a househusband, plus the unadulterated envy of all her workmates. It works for them. It sounds great. She admits to feeling guilty now and again, but so do most businesswomen with kids.

The options are numerous: crêche, childminder, nanny, job-sharing, part-time, flexitime or full-time work, working from home, etc. If you can access all options then the choice is yours and it may well be down to emotions and need, rather than logic or assumption.

- You currently have the right to 18 weeks paid maternity leave. In 2003 it rises to 26 weeks.

- Fathers don't have a right yet. In 2003 they can have two weeks paid leave at £100 per week.

Useful websites:

- Parents at Work (www.parentsatwork.org.uk)
- Mumsnet (www.mumsnet.com)
- iVillage (www.ivillage.co.uk)

Dating

One of the biggest casualties of longer working hours has been the good, old-fashioned pick-up. Like everything else in our time-beleaguered lives, going on the pull and the subsequent first few dates have proved to be more than our groaning diaries can cope with. Even blind dates prove hugely time-inefficient in terms of effort v outcome. I know many single people who claim to have shunned the whole process of dating because it is too inefficient and wastes whole swathes of time.

Time-efficient pulling

So how can you make the pick-up process speedier? Just keep one thought in mind before you apply the following tips: most couples I know didn't fancy one another when they first met. It took time for them to fall in lust and love. If you stereotype 'the kind of person I like' then you may be missing out. Opposites can attract. Ugly ducklings turn out to be swans. Keep a bit of an open mind if you can.

OK, then, here are some of the nippiest ways to find a partner:

Date someone from work

Advantages:

- It's convenient.

- ◆ You get to watch him or her in a whole range of situations before deciding to date.

- ◆ You speak the same jargon.

- ◆ You have something in common.

- ◆ You have time to look beyond the stereotype.

- ◆ You have time to make yourself appear attractive, witty and interesting.

- ◆ You have time to make him/her fall in love with you, even if he/she didn't consider you to be his/her type initially.

- ◆ You can date someone you are friends with.

- ◆ You can make friends with someone you want to date.

- ◆ You share common goals and mission statements.

- ◆ You both work late together.

- ◆ Going for a drink straight from work is less tiring than rushing home and changing to go out on a date.

Disadvantages:

- ◆ You will be gossiped about.

- ◆ You will find it harder to get rid of him/her if it doesn't work out.

- ◆ If he/she jilts you your humiliation will be public.

- ◆ You will have to see him/her again every day if you are lovelorn.

- ◆ Your work could suffer.

- ◆ Your reputation or career could suffer.

Dating from a supermarket

This is one way of 'double-bagging', i.e. saving time by doing two jobs at once. Supermarkets are becoming the hottest place to pull and some chains have even tried to cash in on the idea by introducing 'singles nights'.

Advantages:

◆ Convenience.

◆ It's fun.

Disadvantage:

◆ Do you really want him/her to see you filling your trolley with Harpic, cat food and facial hair removing cream?

Internet dating

Advantages:

◆ You get to chat before you meet.

◆ No visual stereotyping – you fall for one another via words before you meet.

Disadvantages:

These are so obvious and so well documented by the press and various soap plots that they are barely worth mentioning, but:

◆ You have no idea how old, ugly or grotesque your date is before you meet.

◆ You have no idea how much of a pervert or liar he/she is.

◆ The photos they send will be unrealistic.

It's probably better to keep the communication on a pen-pals basis and never, ever meet.

Blind dates

You network in business, so why not network to find your soul mate? After all, who knows you better than your best friends and who would be better placed to recommend and set up a date with a potential life partner?

Well, probably a one-eyed ape is the answer. Blind dates spell disaster. They are the original example of hope and optimism triumphing over experience. Your friends will only ever set you up with a monster because:

♦ They will want to keep anything with remote potential on ice for themselves, even if they are already in a relationship because the whole thing might turn pear-shaped.

♦ They know this man/woman really well and feel sorry for them.

♦ They only see him/her through the eyes of someone who isn't going to be expected to have sex with this person.

♦ They have tried to warn you that this person has a lovely voice/personality but you were too excited by the prospect of a date to read between the lines and listen to what they were really trying to tell you.

♦ Friendship creates blindness.

Go, go, go on these things, though, even if they hurt. At least you can assume the other person is single and not a child molester. You never know where the next Mr D'Arcy is coming from. The pain might be worth it. And at least you get to 'double-bag' and see your friends at the same time.

Dating agencies

When I was younger there was always a full-page ad for these things in any newspaper. It asked you to fill in a questionnaire to find the perfect mate. We all filled them in for fun at some time or another and then laughed at the sad types who would actually put the thing in an envelope and stick it in the post in the hope of finding Mr or Ms Right.

Now I find nearly all my single friends use dating agencies regularly. They are the new social success story. Professional types of a certain age who are coming out of their first or maybe even third marriage and have neither the time nor the inclination to go out on the pull are turning to them in droves, and why not? Like everything else in the well-off business person's life, there's nothing that can't be delegated. Hire an agent and let them take over the first stages of matchmaking. You'd do the same for business recruitment, so why not for partnership? The cost can be alarming, but what price love? And most of the agencies will tell you that they keep their charges high to eliminate the time-wasters or low-salaried.

Advantages:

◆ Professionalism.

◆ Speed.

◆ Some attempt to pick the right mate with the right things in common has been made for you.

◆ You may get to see photos or even a video.

Disadvantages:

◆ Expensive.

◆ Varying quality of the agencies.

◆ Embarrassment at the idea of dating a virtual stranger.

◆ The cost may mean that he/she gets a guaranteed number of dates for his/her money. Even if you click on the first date your partner may feel obliged to go the full length of the counter just to make sure he/she's not missing anything. Which means you've got competition.

◆ Still may be some stigma attached to friends knowing how
you met. Some couples are open about it, others keep quiet.

Speed dating

Some dating agencies have taken time management and turned it
into an art form. Speed dating has started in the UK and looks like
taking off. The concept is: why waste time on an entire date when
you can probably tell whether the person is right for you in as
little as the first ten minutes? Singletons work their way around a
room full of members of the opposite sex, chatting at small tables
for two until their ten minutes are up, when they get up and
move on to the next table.

Advantage:

◆ Speed.

Disadvantages:

◆ Trying to sell yourself in ten minutes and trying to keep an
open mind when that is all the time you have to assess the
other person.

◆ Hoping you click with somebody, but facing potential
disappointment if you are left a wallflower.

Time Logging Your Marriage and Family

Marriages and families are horribly time-consuming unless you
work as a team, in which case they can save time. I know one
couple who work well as a team. She does all the jobs he's not
good at and vice versa. When they do dinner parties they both
cook and, miraculously, they move like a well-oiled machine.
Even their kids are getting to the stage where they fall into the
chores. And even they are falling in seamlessly. There's been no

nagging or bullying for this to happen. They just all seem to realise very early on that conflict is counter-productive and that teams do things better.

Team building

Rate your family as a team. How do they perform? Are you time constructive or time destructive? If you can do it without anyone seeing, try a family time log. How much time is wasted arguing, bickering or doing nothing, just to keep the peace? How much time is wasted over each family task? How fair is the delegation? If you managed this team, what would you see as its weaknesses and strengths?

Write a list of your family team's main problems. What prevents it being time-efficient, problem-solving and objective-achieving? (Expect this list to take a lot of thinking time to produce.) Now write down actions for improvement. Be non-involved when you do this. This is not a 'he/she's wrong and I'm right' list, it's a forward-moving action plan that involves everyone.

One of the big improvements in family team building is exactly the same as work-team issues. People are motivated by praise and recognition. It comes up top on most 'What motivates you the most?' research lists. At home we often opt for the 'Taking them for granted' strategy. Try looking for areas of praise and thanks, instead.

Learn to say sorry

Much time is lost in home rows where one or both parties just refuse to say one word: 'sorry'. As a rule the British love to apologise for things we haven't done but refuse point blank to apologise for things that we have done.

'Sorry' is a lot quicker than counter-accusations. But it should never sound like: 'I'm sorry, OK?' or 'I said I'm sorry what more do you want?'

Listen

Being able to listen is often an underused skill at home. Assumption comes as a result of over-familiarity. You begin by finishing off one another's sentences and you end by feeling you don't need to be listening at all. You already know what they have got to say.

Not being listened to is annoying and insulting. Almost worse is having someone go through the motions of pretending to listen to you because you have pointed out that they never do.

Good relationships need empathy and perception, not emotional blindness. To know someone well you need to listen to their words *and* read between the lines, too. If your partner tells you they are unhappy or depressed you need to discuss the issues that have caused those feelings. If you don't then their behaviour may change but their feelings might not. They will be masking in an attempt to re-create equilibrium. Feelings that are stored away tend to fester, though. Instead of healing at source you may end up dealing with a divorce. Talk and discuss, don't bury under the carpet.

Quality Time

Deciding to spend more time with your partner can be an eerie experience. When one of a couple who is usually absent suddenly appears in the lounge, staring at the other and trying to make conversation the result is usually mayhem. So be careful how you structure your work–life balancing changes of routine if that is the path you are bent on following. The result of this kind of generous lending of precious time, known sickeningly as 'quality time', is usually one or all of the following:

◆ Your partner thinks you are about to confess to an affair.

◆ Your partner confesses to an affair.

◆ You start catching up on arguments you have not previously had time to have.

♦ One of you thinks 'quality time' means more sex and the other believes it means more in-depth chats.

Don't expect to be welcomed like the Prodigal Son just because you've decided to balance your time better and work shorter hours. It could be that your partner – despite constant moaning that you work too late – has formed his or her own social routine that is quite comfortable. Perhaps you will be seen as upsetting the equilibrium. Expect to have to wean yourself into the household routine slowly and tactfully, rather than riding in on a chariot and expecting all the troops to cheer.

If you have been an absent partner for too long you may also find problems with the hierarchy when you return to the bosom of the fold. If your partner has been master of all they survey they may not take kindly to someone else ordering the troops about. The troops themselves may mutiny at the new leadership responsibilities.

♦ Never be critical about the way things have been running in your absence.

♦ Never try to reorganise things like shopping trips or children's bedtimes.

♦ Do ask to help.

♦ Do start by offering affection and romance, rather than 'banging-your-head-on-the-headboard' sex.

♦ Do take up a hobby of your own, preferably one that keeps you in sight of the house.

♦ Do keep talk about work and the characters involved down to a minimum.

♦ Do go shopping together but don't get too clever. There is something monstrous about the sight of men accompanying their wives around shops like BHS and joining in with too much enthusiasm while their wives try clothes on.

Whether you are realigning your home time or not, it is helpful to do a swift and relatively casual time log of your marriage or live-together relationship.

See how long you spend on negative rituals, like moaning about work, moaning about one another and arguing. If you argue excessively, try to discover all the prompts and themes of the arguments. Many of them will be serial arguments, i.e. constant, unresolved battles over the same issues. The stimulus will often be the same and so will the response. These things tend to run in patterns and the longer they go on the harder they are to resolve. See if there is any way that you can break this pattern of behaviour. Don't expect your partner to change, it is you who have chosen to read this book and you who – I hope – has decided that life is too short to wage war over who put the empty milk bottle back in the fridge. Either change your stimulus or change your response. Break the ties. Do something different. But make it something better.

Lifestyle Managers

Don't you just *want* one of these, even if you don't know what they are?

The thought of having someone to 'remove all the irritations of domestic life' is like nectar to any wannabe time-manager.

These people are the latest perk for high-fliers, who are so busy saving the world that they both need and deserve someone to take care of tasks like organising holidays, booking plumbers and repairmen and even shopping for family birthdays. You fill in a questionnaire with your likes and dislikes and then pay a monthly fee, and then ring with your needs and wants. I couldn't think of anything better, although several people I suggested the service to said they already had one of these for free, called the wife or the husband or the secretary.

One time-management step I would never recommend is using your secretary to manage your private chores. This is so cheeky it should be made illegal.

I find my least-liked tasks all come under the heading of 'booking' things, like decorators and dental appointments. Having someone to deal with these and other emergencies sounds like a dream. Evidentially they cost out at around £100 per month – a fantastic delegating opportunity if you can afford it.

If you don't want to find your own agency, perhaps your company will provide one for you. The head of human resources at the UBS investment bank was quoted as saying recently: 'Now we realise that the most important asset is the employees. If they need services and we can provide them, that's what we need to do.' Their service provider, Enviego, will do anything from finding a dog walker to calling in a plumber or booking tables in restaurants like The Ivy.

If you don't use a lifestyle manager, perhaps you could take advantage of some of the 'to your door' office services on offer. You can buy almost anything from the comfort of your own desk these days, from sandwiches to books to CDs to shirts. You can have a massage or a facial and you can have your dry-cleaning collected and delivered.

Keeping Fit

Fitness regimes can vary tremendously in terms of dedicated time spent. You don't need to spend hours at the gym or working out with a personal trainer – as little as half an hour of fast walking a day can make a difference.

If you intend building vast wedges of training time into your day you need to have clear objectives. Are you exercising to:

1. Lose weight? A diet will be more effective, combined with some light exercise. Exercise alone will not be enough to get the pounds off, in fact some exercise regimes actually build bulk up.

2. As a social hobby? Many people go to the gym to meet friends and socialise.

3. To get fit? If this is your aim, make sure you include aerobic

exercise. Weight training will build muscle but not always improve overall fitness. Make sure you don't overdo the training. It is possible to become obsessive. Unless you are training towards some peak achievement, like a marathon, keep your training within the bounds of enjoyment. Gym workouts are more effective if you go after work than before. In a study at the University of Chicago, blood samples taken showed that levels of two endocrine hormones increased far more in those who exercised either in the evening or late at night. Leading researcher Dr Orfeu Buxton says: 'There are signs that your metabolism is adapting well to regular exercise and suggests it may be better to train after work rather than first thing in the morning.'

Planning Your Social Diary

This may need to be dealt with as ferociously as your business diary. A lot will depend on how much you like your out-of-work time to be planned at all. Perhaps you prefer to leave two-day gaps and see what happens. Or maybe your life is one structured social whirl. Then again, perhaps it is a mix of both. If you err towards the 'whirl' side you may need to plan some time of inactivity and guard it ferociously.

Turning down social invitations to spend precious time doing things you want to do is difficult. Nobody likes being told that their magnanimous invite to their party or dinner is being refused. Which is why we usually resort to lying.

Being assertive means being honest. Being honest about turning an invite down is not always the best policy, though. 'Thank you, but I'd rather stick needles in my eyes' will only cause hurt and conflict, as will 'I nearly died of boredom last time' or 'I couldn't stand another bout with your groper of a husband'.

If you decide to lie, then do so cleverly. Bad liars fall into three traps:

1. Overdoing their regrets, as in:

You say: 'We are *absolutely devastated* to be missing your summer barbecue. It was the highlight of our social calendar last year. We'd do anything to be there, but Sophie's mother has got this triple heart bypass and . . .'

They say: 'Don't worry, we'll reschedule for the weekend after.'

2. Saying you'll go but not turning up and then pretending something came up at the last minute. This is probably the worst option because parties often suffer from a multiple case of this one, leaving the poor hosts staring at acres of untouched fondue.

3. Saying your kid was taken sick. I was always told God punishes liars by turning the lie into reality.

Making your excuses

You do need to close this one down with a lie that is both convincing and, hopefully, ensures you won't get asked to the next party. Keep your excuses concise, as long rambling storylines with too much elaboration will always be a giveaway. Try something like: 'No thanks, we're not really party animals' or tell them you are booked up for that evening, but without going into details where.

People who push the point and try to insist you come are really being rude. This is where you will have to fall back on the 'broken record' technique of repeating your point in the face of excessive persuasion. Keep to your bottom line, be polite but be firm, as in: 'I'm sorry, no . . . No, I'm afraid we just can't make it . . . No, I'm sorry.'

'Double-bag' like crazy with your own friends. A big dinner party is not much more effort than a small one so invite heaps of friends and help prevent a long line of smaller parties.

House Hopping

Many people buy second properties in a bid to clarify their out-of-work hours. These country homes became an idyll, a sea of tranquillity far from the city bustle. Many bought abroad, and France became very popular. The idea was to achieve balance and rest. If the idea worked I would include it in my recommendations for time management, because a weekend of rest and repair is the perfect solution to brain burn-out. But for many it didn't. The properties became a millstone for many. They cost money, so they had to be used. Instead of returning home knackered on a Friday night to nothing more strenuous than reaching for the remote control and ordering a takeaway pizza, business couples were going through a frenzied ritual of late-night shopping, packing, gagging the kids, clingfilming the cat and then Cresta-run-style midnight driving up to cold cottages in Norfolk (if you are lucky) and the Peak District (if you are not). The properties threw up new realms of DIY, needing constant weeding, wall building and roofing repairs. Pets ran off to frolic in the fields with the bunnies and only returned at 2.00am Monday morning.

A weekend 'retreat' is usually anything but. I only know one couple who ever achieved the kind of blissful sanctuary that we all dream of, and they put in a lot of hard work and kept a strict routine about their visits.

Weekend Guests

Then there is the added time-horror of visitors. You find yourself inviting every man and his dog to come and stay and often they all do, and usually all at once. Whereas a visit in town will mean hosting for a four-hour stretch, max, country-cottage visits mean donning the mine-host hat for up to three days at a time. You will die of exhaustion. Guests treat the place as a holiday home, turning up clutching nothing better than petrol-station flowers, lying in late, keeping you up past midnight, drinking all your wine and going for walks when the washing up is being done. (I don't have a weekend retreat but I have been a house guest.)

The answer is to invest in an inner-city pad. Smart property-owners wanting a change of scene at weekends buy in other parts of town. A friend of mine who is an estate agent lives with her partner near Islington but has her 'country' property by the Thames in Docklands. The flat is small but the view is great. They go for walks by the river and they don't have a phone there. The drive takes ten minutes, which maximises relaxation time. Bliss.

CHAPTER TWENTY-THREE

Summary

Try to take your time-management cut with a large chunk of fun. Being too serious about your schedule means losing the greater part of the quality of life.

Expect to be busy and expect to get bored. That rotation works well, because we look forward to 'busy' when we're bored, and ache for a period of bored when we are rushed off our feet. It's when the 'busy' turns into 'can't cope' that we need to worry. It's when life is all moving too quickly that we need to start some major pruning and rearranging the furniture to create a few gaps.

Don't lose your sense of humour.

Don't fail to seek out the important things in your life, whatever they might be.

Do work through the 'now' with an eye firmly on the 'where I want to be'.

Digging time holes is hard work. You need to dig like crazy and then protect each gap. They will be empty but that is to allow the unexpected good stuff, the brilliant stuff of life to fall in. Never allow those holes to refill with more sand. Dig and then protect. That is what this book has been all about.

Index